What Others Are Saying
Why Social Justice Is Not Biblical Justice

This book is an eye-opening, insightful, and (to my mind) truthful warning about the deeply anti-Christian ideas behind much of the modern "social justice" movement, a movement that insists on dividing all of society into the oppressors (people of privilege who can do nothing good) and the oppressed (people who can do nothing evil). By contrast, Scott Allen firmly grounds his argument in biblical ideas of justice. He does not hesitate to name specific people and evangelical organizations that are in danger of being led astray by following contemporary calls for social justice instead of true biblical justice. Highly recommended!

Wayne Grudem, PhD
Distinguished Research Professor of Theology and Biblical Studies
Phoenix Seminary

We are a wounded nation now, and Christians need to bind up wounds and not make new ones. Instead of scorning those who push for social justice, we should recognize that leftist ideologues have twisted the concept—and some Christians have naively gone along with the distortion. Scott Allen offers an alternative that's crucial to consider. My own sense is that there is an alternative: Churches and organizations should foster and spotlight compassionate approaches that help people rise out of poverty. We should be discerning about programs that sound good but build class, racial, and cultural antagonism. If we are unable to reclaim the biblical understanding of justice, we'll end up with just ice.

Marvin Olasky
Editor in chief of *WORLD* magazine

Scott Allen carefully reveals how "ideological social justice" is a new religious replacement for the Judeo-Christian worldview. If we allow its social engineers to succeed, both the church and the world will suffer immeasurably. No longer will human beings have a basis of unalienable rights, intrinsic worth, and freedom to flourish. Only biblical truth is true love. I urge you to read and share this book immediately and widely!

Kelly Monroe Kullberg
Author of *Finding God Beyond Harvard: The Quest for Veritas*
Founder and former executive director of the Veritas Forum

The modern social justice movement is a Trojan horse that is being welcomed into many evangelical camps with the kind of fanfare that would make the citizens of Troy blush. Under the pretense of loving one's neighbor and pursuing justice, ideologies that are contrary to the way of Christ are being employed to set agendas for and shape the consciences of evangelicals. Because biblical words are being used, what the Bible means by those words is assumed and that assumption is wreaking havoc on sound Christian thinking and healthy Christian living. Scott Allen understands this and has done all Christians a great service by revealing what's inside the horse. By tracing the history of the neo-Marxist and postmodern ideologies that are driving the social justice movement, Allen exposes its deconstructive agenda and ungodly methods. More importantly, he gives a helpful overview of genuine justice as revealed by the just God in the Holy Scriptures. We have long needed a book like this. Every serious Christian— especially every pastor—should read and heed the wisdom it contains.

Tom Ascol
Senior pastor of Grace Baptist Church (Cape Coral, Florida)
President of Founders Ministries

Scott Allen's insight into the dangerous present situation the church finds itself in is much needed and could not have come at a better moment! Christians do not have the option of sitting on the fence while both the gospel and biblical law are corrupted. It's time for Bereans to compare what they're hearing, even from pastors, to God's revelation. Allen is able to break down the ethical assumptions behind social justice theory and provide and explain a biblical and Christian alternative. Digest every page!

Jon Harris
Host, *Conversations That Matter* Podcast

The life-or-death tone that permeates this book is there for good reason. If the present course is not altered, the consequences will not just be a fully fractured "evangelicalism." It could mean twenty-first-century gulags, guillotines, or death camps. Overstated? Judge for yourself. Read this book! Scott Allen is not just providing a well-documented, much-needed analysis. He is blowing a trumpet, not only by clarifying what a biblically informed Christ-follower must be against, but what a biblically informed Christ-follower must be for.

Christian Overman, PhD
Author of *Assumptions That Affect Our Lives* and *God's Pleasure at Work*

Scott Allen's book deals with the ideology of the social justice movement. Many who understand the need for justice in society have affirmed the policies and practices of this movement without examining the set of ideas from which it emanates. Others have felt uncomfortable with the tenants of the movement but not understood why. Movements are born out of a set of principles and paradigm and will inevitably lead to certain policies and practices. Everyone who has an interest in justice or in what is taking place in society would do well to read this book. Scott, who has dedicated his life to fighting poverty, hunger, and injustice, has done us all a service in reflecting on the biblical concept of justice in comparison with the ideology of social justice.

Darrow L. Miller
Author of *Discipling Nations: The Power of Truth to Transform Culture*
Cofounder of the Disciple Nations Alliance

Earnest Christians, eager to rectify ancient wrongs, are being seduced by an antibiblical worldview that masquerades as social justice. Scott Allen's bold and compelling thesis exposes this fatal seduction with the wisdom and grace that magnifies the glorious vision of truly biblical justice. Lest we take seriously this wake-up call, Christians are likely to either slumber toward judgment or to thrash about in manic activism that fails our neighbors and our God.

Bob Osburn, PhD
Founder and executive director of Wilberforce Academy

Scott Allen draws a very significant distinction between secular social justice and justice as taught in Scripture. He shows how secular social justice arose, how it is widely influential, and how it has had devastating effects on our society. He clearly demonstrates that this secular version is alien to biblical justice. I recommend this work to anyone in ministry. It will help you think deeply about what true justice is and how secular social justice leads us astray from the gospel.

Rev. Ernest B. Manges, PhD
Professor of theology and church history, Cebu Graduate School of Theology,
Philippines

Scott has logically unpacked this crucial issue in a way that is sensitive, thorough, yet accessible and nonacademic. I will share this book with anyone who will take the time to read it. It is both urgent and outstanding!

Bob Moffitt
Author of *If Jesus Were Mayor: How Your Local Church Can Transform Your Community*
President of the Harvest Foundation

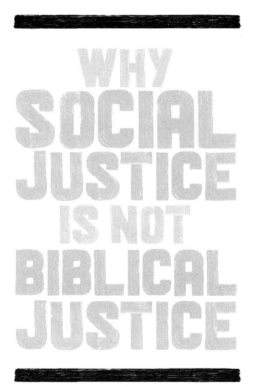

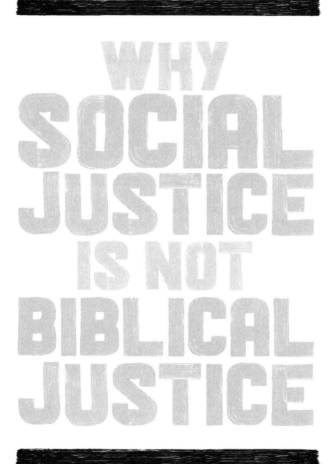

WHY SOCIAL JUSTICE IS NOT BIBLICAL JUSTICE

AN URGENT APPEAL TO FELLOW CHRISTIANS IN A TIME OF SOCIAL CRISIS

SCOTT DAVID ALLEN

credo
house publishers

Published in the United States of America by Credo House Publishers,
a division of Credo Communications, LLC, Grand Rapids, Michigan
credohousepublishers.com

ISBN: 978-1-62586-176-4

Cover and interior design by Frank Gutbrod
Editing by Elizabeth Banks and Stan Guthrie

Printed in the United States of America

First edition

Your throne, O God, will last for ever and ever;
a scepter of justice will be the scepter of your kingdom;
You love righteousness and hate wickedness.

—Psalm 45:6–7

BIBLICAL JUSTICE

Conformity to God's moral standard as revealed in the Ten Commandments and the Royal Law: "love your neighbor as yourself."

Communitive justice: living in right relationship with God and others; giving people their due as image-bearers of God.

Distributive justice: impartially rendering judgment, righting wrongs, and meting out punishment for lawbreaking. Reserved for God and God-ordained authorities including parents in the home, elders in the church, teachers in the school, and civil authorities in the state.

SOCIAL JUSTICE

Deconstructing traditional systems and structures deemed to be oppressive, and redistributing power and resources from oppressors to their victims in the pursuit of equality of outcome.

CONTENTS

INTRODUCTION

> According to the biblical worldview, people "are children of God, fashioned in His divine image. [According to] Social Justice, we are children of society, fashioned by its social constructions and the power dynamics they maintain."
> —James A. Lindsay and Mike Nayna
> "Postmodern Religion and the Faith of Social Justice"

> Cultural engagement without cultural discernment leads to cultural captivity.
> —Ken Meyers

In recent years, a powerful ideology has made deep inroads into the very heart of the evangelical church. To its mainstream advocates, it is called "social justice" and is nearly always coupled with a commitment to equality, diversity, and inclusion.

Christians of all stripes also share a deep commitment to justice, as well as to equality, diversity, and inclusion. Yet as John Stonestreet, president of the Colson Center for Christian Worldview, is fond of saying, "It's no good having the same vocabulary if we're using different dictionaries."[1]

So true. What cultural advocates of social justice mean by these words, as we will see, is completely different from the way they are defined in Scripture and how they have been historically understood in Western culture.

Words matter. They shape our ideas and form our belief systems. These belief systems, in turn, drive our culture, which shapes how we think and behave, for good or bad. Most people take words for granted. We use them but rarely take time to think about them, unaware of their incredible power. All cultural change begins with language change. Changes in language— new words, new definitions—can usually be traced to powerful thought leaders who may have lived hundreds of years before.

The late Christian philosopher Dallas Willard wrote, "The ideas of economists and political philosophers, both when they are right and when they are wrong, are more powerful than is commonly understood. Indeed, the world is ruled by little else."[2]

God raised up the church to advance His kingdom of goodness, light, and beauty into this fallen world. One of the most important ways we do this is by communicating and embodying the powerful, life-giving words of God in Scripture—words such as freedom, love, compassion, and *justice*.

The Bible is far more than a message of salvation, as absolutely vital as that is. It is a comprehensive worldview that defines and shapes all aspects of reality and human existence. It is God's "Transforming Story," but unlike other worldviews, it is *true*. It accords with reality as it actually exists. It defines for all times, and all peoples, what words such as truth, love, justice, and equality actually mean. These true, biblical definitions give rise to distinctively Christian cultures. In the words of theologian Robert Lewis Wilken, "culture lives by language, and the sentiments, thoughts, and feelings of a Christian culture are formed and carried by the language of the Scriptures."[3]

So, when the evangelical church intentionally or unintentionally exchanges the biblical definition of a word as important as *justice* with a counterfeit, it is no small matter.

Ideas have consequences, but as Os Guinness reminds us, they also have antecedents—that is, they come from somewhere. The true definition of justice finds its source in the Bible and has expressed itself historically in ways that have blessed nations. Yet today we take all this for granted, including the rule of law and due process.

The counterfeit is sourced in "hollow and deceptive" philosophies (Colossians 2:8) that emerged in Europe in the 1700s. It traces its lineage back to famous philosophers and activists such as Immanuel Kant, Friedrich Nietzsche, Karl Marx, Antonio Gramsci, and Michel Foucault. Their ideas have taken deep root in Western culture. Over time, they have mutated and merged into a school of thought that contemporary academics call *critical theory*. Other names include identity politics, intersectionality, or cultural Marxism. However, in this book, I refer to it as *ideological social justice*. I use the modifier "ideological" to indicate that we are discussing something much bigger than justice. Rather, it is a comprehensive ideology, or worldview, which helps to explain why it is attracting so many adherents.

We need worldviews to make sense of our lives. They help us understand our identity and purpose. In our increasingly post-Christian society, a growing number of people have no knowledge of the Bible, yet it was the biblical worldview that shaped the West for centuries. It provided the basic assumptions that supplied many generations with their identity and purpose, whether they were Christians or not. But today, with the Bible and the biblical worldview in rapid decline, ideological social justice is filling the vacuum.

Our worldviews determine not only how we think, but how we act. They drive the choices we make. They act like the roots of a fruit tree. The roots determine the fruit. Speaking of false teachers and deceitful ideologies, Jesus said, "By their fruit you will recognize them" (Matthew 7:16). As you will see in this book, ideological social justice can be recognized by its bitter fruit. The lives and cultures shaped by it are marked by enmity, hostility, suspicion, entitlement, and grievance.

Tragically, this false worldview is making deep inroads into the evangelical church, which is in grave danger of abandoning true justice for an imposter.

I believe this exchange is happening mostly unintentionally. Ideological social justice has poured forth from the universities and into the broader culture with such speed and force over the past thirty years that all of us have been affected to one degree or another. Today it is the dominant worldview shaping vast swaths of the culture. Ten years ago, it was largely confined to university humanities programs. Now it is the reigning worldview throughout nearly every aspect of education, both K-12 and higher education. It dominates big business, the media, entertainment, high tech, and much of our government, including our systems of justice. In the words of essayist and cultural critic Andrew Sullivan, "we all live on campus now."[4]

Christians are certainly not immune to such powerful ideas, which shape the institutions we all share. Many Christians have largely absorbed the assumptions of ideological social justice unawares. After all, it uses biblical words and concepts such as justice, oppression, antiracism, and equality—yet it stealthily redefines them all.

To recognize a counterfeit, you have to first know the genuine article. So I begin this book by conveying what biblical justice is before examining ideological social justice. I will hold them up, side by side, in hope that a comparison of their key differences will foster clarity in the midst of all the confusion that seems to reign among evangelicals.

I've had a passion for this subject ever since God called me into full-time vocational ministry during my senior year in college in 1988. That year, I joined the international Christian relief and development organization Food for the Hungry as a cross-cultural community development worker.

In 1988, the evangelical church was starkly divided over justice, which, at the time, was typically equated with concern for the poor and marginalized. On one side of this divide were theological conservatives who held to a more literal interpretation of Scripture and viewed the goal of Christian missions as gospel proclamation and church planting. They were suspicious about ministry to the poor because of its past association with the heretical "social gospel."

On the other side was a smaller group of evangelical activists who cared deeply about poverty and justice. One of their most prominent leaders, Ron Sider of Eastern Theological Seminary in Philadelphia, published his influential book *Rich Christians in an Age of Hunger* in 1978 and later founded Evangelicals for Social Action. Another leader, Jim Wallis, founded *Sojourners* in 1971. Personally, I was drawn to these men and their movement.

My twenty years of work with Food for the Hungry took me to some of the poorest nations on earth. Over these years,

I deepened my knowledge about the causes of and solutions to poverty, and the more I learned, the less enthusiastic I became about my former beliefs.

When I started my career at Food for the Hungry, I had just graduated from one of Oregon's well-known private liberal arts universities. I didn't identify as a Marxist, but I had absorbed a hefty dose of Marxist ideology from my professors and fellow students. I largely assumed that wealth and resources were zero-sum—those who had them had come by them illegitimately, at the expense of those who didn't. Wealthy nations acquired their riches through colonialism, greed, and rapacious capitalism. They had gamed the system at the expense of the poor. It took many years, with the help of some wonderful, godly mentors, before I fully realized my assumptions about wealth and poverty were rooted more in the Communist Manifesto than the Bible.

Ultimately, I had to ask myself this question: Was I more interested in wealth disparities and income redistribution, or in doing what has proven to be effective in actually empowering people to rise from poverty?

Over time I came to see that Marxist worldview assumptions do far more to harm the poor than to help them. It did not see the poor as fully human, created in the image of God, with dignity, responsibility, and the capacity to create new wealth and new opportunities. My former Marxist-influenced worldview saw them largely as helpless victims, dependent upon the actions of beneficent Westerners to overcome poverty. This fostered a destructive sense of paternalism and guilt on one side, and a damaging sense of dependency and entitlement on the other.

Looking back on history, and our own Christian heritage, I discovered times when God worked through the church to lift entire nations out of poverty. Before the Reformation, for example, the nations of northern Europe were as impoverished as the nations of Africa are today. After the Reformation, they began to prosper. This transformation didn't come about because of wealth redistribution, enlightened human wisdom, or scientific or technical know-how. It happened because people began to open the Bible, and to understand reality, including their own identity and purpose, in new and life-changing ways. It was the power of biblical truth—of the biblical worldview—that lifted people out of poverty and built free, prosperous nations.

The passion to share this insight led me and my close friends Darrow Miller and Bob Moffitt to launch the Disciple Nations Alliance in 1997. Our mission was to catalyze a Christian movement that would call the church back to a comprehensive biblical worldview, and to proclaim and demonstrate the power of biblical truth in ways that lead to positive change, particularly among the poor.

To the conservative wing of the evangelical church, our message was this: Your passion for the gospel is good and praiseworthy! But gospel proclamation is only the beginning of genuine Christian mission, not the end. Once saved, Christians must be carefully discipled to recognize and replace false cultural assumptions with the biblical worldview, and then to bring the truth, goodness, and beauty of God's kingdom into every sphere of our broken nations. God's plan of redemption isn't limited to saving souls. It encompasses the reconciliation of all forms of broken relationships: with God, with ourselves, with our fellow human beings, and with creation itself. There should be no divide between gospel proclamation, discipleship, church planting, and social and cultural transformation. These are all essential aspects of our overall mission. "Wholistic mission" or "wholistic ministry" became the buzzwords and shorthand labels we used to describe this comprehensive view of Christian ministry.

To the social justice wing of the evangelical church, our message was this: If you truly want to empower the impoverished to rise, the most potent tool at your disposal is biblical truth and compassion.[5] Poverty isn't ultimately rooted in unjust systems but in satanic deception at the level of culture. A Christian approach to social change must focus on witnessing to the truth in all realms of human existence. When rich and poor alike begin to replace cultural lies with biblical truth, transformation happens. This transformation is never complete or uniform or indefinite, but it is real, powerful, God-honoring, and significant.

Over the last twenty-three years, as we and others have been sharing similar teachings, we've seen many signs of positive change. On the conservative side, we've seen a tremendous embrace of a wholistic approach to mission. Among those Christian groups and organizations working to uplift the poor, we've seen a real receptivity to the idea that discipleship in a biblical worldview is the most powerful thing we can do to uplift impoverished communities.

As both sides began to change, our hope grew that the old evangelical divide could be bridged and a new, God-honoring unity forged. There were many encouraging signs that this was, indeed, happening.

But then, seemingly out of nowhere, Marxist presuppositions were back in a big way, influencing a new generation of evangelical leaders in a different guise, and threatening to undermine the growing unity. Talk of "social justice" was everywhere in evangelical circles. But unlike the 1980s, the focus was less on poverty, and more on race, sex, gender, and sexual orientation. In 2010, a dynamic young pastor from Oregon named Ken Wytsma launched the Justice Conference, which was tremendously influential among millennial evangelicals. Based on what I read in Ken's book *The Myth of Equality* and heard from the speakers at his conferences, he seemed to be offering a potent cocktail that was two parts biblical theology and one-part academic critical theory.

My alarm grew when I saw this same syncretism spreading into the very heart of mainstream evangelicalism.

This all became quite personal in 2018 when a few close, respected evangelical colleagues began to challenge me: Wasn't I aware of the pervasive structural racism and oppression in America? Didn't I recognize my culpability in that oppression? Hadn't I come to grips with my inherent privilege and unconscious racism?

WHAT WAS GOING ON?

This is a dangerous moment. If current trends continue, the evangelical church will be rapidly syncretized into a profoundly destructive and unbiblical ideology that will do incalculable harm to its mission and witness in this world.

Justice is one of the most important words in the Bible. It is one of the most important concepts in any culture. If the Bible-believing church abandons genuine justice in favor of a destructive cultural counterfeit, who will be left to uphold and defend the truth? The stakes are very high.

My fervent prayer is that this book will help serve as a wake-up call to my evangelical brothers and sisters. This is my plea: Recognize and reject the counterfeit. Remember what true justice is. Hold fast to that truth, no matter how unpopular. Speak it out. Demonstrate it. Be the salt and light Jesus commands us to be.

Each generation of Christians must uphold and defend the truth and pass it on to future generations, including the truth about justice. Here is my small and imperfect attempt to do so.

One final word before we jump in. In researching for this book, I've read widely in my attempt to better understand academic critical theory, often from its many influential popularizers. I've had numerous iron-sharpening-iron discussions with people who firmly disagree with the positions I take in this book—nearly all who I count as friends, and brothers and sisters in Christ. To you, I would like to say this: I deeply value your friendship. I share your deep passion and commitment for justice, and your desire to be a voice for the voiceless and to uphold the cause of the poor and the oppressed. While I've developed strong convictions on these topics, I have much to learn and undoubtedly have unbiblical perspectives that need correcting. For this reason, I need your friendship more than ever.

Please do not take our disagreement as hostility or condemnation on my part. While I hate false, destructive ideas, I desire to love and show respect to the people who hold them. I've had (and still have) my fair share of false beliefs and am eternally grateful for those who love me enough to help me see them. I want to do the same for others. I have logs in my own eyes that need to be removed. I need your help seeing them. I also want to be the kind of person who loves others enough to help them remove the logs from their eyes as well. This is my heart.

Scott Allen
July 2020

CHAPTER 1

STRANGE JUSTICE

oward the end of President Trump's second State of the Union address in February 2019, he turned to the issue of abortion, challenging Americans to "work together to build a culture that cherishes innocent life" and to "reaffirm a fundamental truth: All children, born and unborn, are made in the holy image of God."[1]

Stacey Abrams, a former gubernatorial candidate from Georgia, responded on Twitter, defending the right to a legal abortion by saying, "America achieved a measure of reproductive justice in *Roe v. Wade*."[2] Just what did she mean by "reproductive justice"?

The phrase wasn't hers. It was first coined in 1994 by a group called "Women of African Descent for Reproductive Justice." They defined it this way: "the human right to maintain personal bodily autonomy, have children, not have children, and parent the children we have in safe and sustainable communities."[3]

The notion of "personal bodily autonomy" flows out of postmodernism, which holds that ultimate authority is not vested in God, or in science, but in the autonomous, sovereign individual. And what of the phrase "the right to . . . not have children"? Could this mean the right not to engage in sexual activity that leads to procreation? Hardly. "The right to abort their unborn children" would be a far more accurate expression of the meaning. In other words, "reproductive justice" is the assertion that a mother has the "human right" to take the life of her unborn child if she so chooses.

The irony here is painful. In the days of slavery, the moral reasoning went something like this: Black slaves are not fully human but are the powerless, voiceless property of powerful slave owners to dispose of as they choose. Call it "property justice," if you will. The moral reasoning for abortion is identical. In "reproductive justice," the unborn are not fully human but rather are the powerless, voiceless property of mothers. According to the Women of African Descent for Reproductive Justice, women have the right to exercise their "personal bodily autonomy" by disposing of their unborn as they see fit.

In an appalling irony, this moral reasoning has made abortion the leading cause of death for black lives in America today.[4] Every year, well in excess of *a quarter of a million* unborn black children are lost through abortion.[5] In New York City, more black babies are aborted than are born alive.[6] *This is justice?*

Over the last two hundred years, the West has severed the idea of justice from God and His law, leading to the moral chaos we see today. Instead of relying on a sure and unchanging standard for justice, we are constantly changing standards. What was considered moral five years ago is not only called immoral today but is increasingly ruled illegal. What was considered immoral five years ago—and often was illegal—is now held to be both moral and legal. All of this has opened the door to horrific injustice in the name of justice.

A NEW IDEOLOGY IS EMERGING

Our confusion has perhaps never been greater, both in the church and in the broader culture. A new ideology has emerged that distorts how Americans—Christians included—understand justice. The cultural critic Wesley Yang calls it "the successor ideology" to the older Judeo-Christian worldview that shaped the West and America for centuries. According to *New York Times* editorialist Ross Douthat, it is "inchoate and half-formed and sometimes internally contradictory, defined more by its departures from older liberal ideas than by a unified worldview."[7] Noah Rothman observes that "It influences how businesses structure themselves. It is altering how employers and employees relate to one another. It has utterly transformed academia. [And] it is remaking our politics with alarming swiftness."[8]

Its millions of devotees signal their loyalty to the ideology by speaking proudly of their commitment to "social justice."

Many Christians have only a vague awareness of this ideology and consequently don't see the danger. When they hear "social justice" they assume it is no different than biblical justice. Of course, justice is a deeply biblical idea, but this new ideology is far from biblical. It is, in fact, a comprehensive worldview rooted in Marxist and postmodern presuppositions that competes with a biblical worldview. Today's social justice proponents typically deny the Marxist roots of their worldview (a *Salon* essayist dismissed cultural Marxism as a "hoax concept").[9] To be charitable, we must grant that many of them probably don't even realize the connection. However, a careful examination of social justice and neo-Marxism reveals that they are cut from the same ideological cloth.

Ideas have consequences. True ideas, like biblical justice, are essential building blocks for free, prosperous, and flourishing nations. Bad ideas, like ideological social justice, are terribly destructive, rending the social fabric, exacerbating hostility, and ultimately destroying relationships. It is imperative that Christ-followers, who are called to be ministers of reconciliation (2 Corinthians 5:17–20), carefully discern the difference between biblical justice and the ideology of social justice. Both use the word "justice" but mean vastly different things by it.

Sadly, this kind of wise and careful discernment has been hard to come by. Instead, we are witnessing a growing trend of leading Christian voices wittingly or unwittingly promoting ideological social justice inside the church and sowing confusion by equating it with biblical justice.

I first became aware of this worrisome trend in late 2015 when InterVarsity Christian Fellowship's famous Urbana missions conference in St. Louis invited Michelle Higgins to give a keynote address. She used the opportunity to encourage young mission-minded evangelicals to throw their support behind the Black Lives Matter movement.[10] Higgins did more than promote a message that racism is sinful. She placed support of Black Lives Matter squarely in the mission of God by saying it is "a movement on mission in the truth of God."[11]

Black Lives Matter was founded by three women steeped in neo-Marxist social justice ideology. One of them, Alicia Garza, is a self-described "queer Black woman" who believes that "we must view the epidemic [of black violence] through of a lens of race, gender, sexual orientation, and gender identity."[12] Another, Opal Tometi, describes herself as "transnational feminist" and a "student of liberation theology."[13] The Black Lives Matter mission statement includes a commitment to "disrupt the Western-prescribed nuclear family structure . . . by supporting each other as extended families and 'villages' that collectively care for one another, especially our children."[14]

Of course black lives matter. All lives matter because all lives are made in God's holy image. If that was the extent of the message that InterVarsity was attempting to convey, then fine. But why, by extension, champion a movement founded on such profoundly unbiblical ideas from the main stage of America's premier evangelical missions conference?

Following the conference, the left-leaning evangelical organization *Sojourners* wrote an open letter to InterVarsity, commending the organization for its courage in promoting Black Lives Matter. That letter, penned by Dr. Lawrence A. Q. Burnley, associate vice president for Diversity, Equity and Inclusion at Whitworth University, included this statement:

> Michelle Higgins . . . exposed a central lie at work in the church . . . through her Urbana15 keynote address. The lie is this: White people were created to rule and everyone else was created to be ruled. This lie is the foundation upon which unjust American structures, systems, and policies rest.[15]

In my thirty-five years of working with church leaders around the world, from over seventy-five nations, I've never met anyone who endorsed in any way the idea that "white people were created to rule everyone else." Yet according to this statement, this is the "central lie at work in the church."

Not surprisingly, this statement was endorsed by prominent progressive evangelicals such as Jim Wallis, Shane Claiborne, and Jen Hatmaker. I was, however, surprised to see that it was also signed by more mainstream evangelicals, such as Steve Bauman, president and CEO of World Relief, Lynne Hybels of Chicago's famous Willow Creek Community Church, and David Neff, former editor-in-chief of *Christianity Today*.

Since 1995, ideological social justice has only continued to gain momentum in the broader culture and inside the church. As I began studying this worldview in some depth—where it came from, its basic contours, how it understands reality and human nature, the source of evil and its solution—my concern has only magnified. If the Bible-believing church continued on this trajectory of confusing biblical justice and ideological social justice—of confusing the biblical worldview with this "successor ideology"—how could we be a strong voice for true justice in this morally confused time?

The inroads that ideological social justice is making into the evangelical church need to be recognized and exposed for the good of the church, and the good of the broader society the church exists to serve. Biblical justice is far too important to leave undefended in the face of this stealthy attack from a nonbiblical worldview masking itself behind biblical words and language. This book seeks to remind us, as followers of Jesus Christ, what biblical justice is, and how it differs from social justice. Even more importantly, I want to draw a clear contrast between the presuppositions of a biblical worldview that undergird biblical justice, and the presuppositions that underpin ideological social justice, and how they give rise to a concept of justice that is foreign to the Holy Scriptures and Christian history.

Before we look at the counterfeit, let's spend time reflecting on the incomparable original, the powerful and glorious understanding of justice that flows from the pages of Scripture.

CHAPTER 2

BIBLICAL JUSTICE

The Latin word *justus*, according to Webster's 1828 Dictionary of the American Language,[1] means "straight, or close." Like a plumb line, *justus* refers to a standard or basis *for morality*. Justice is alignment to a standard of goodness. In fact, goodness, or righteousness, is synonymous with justice. Antonyms are injustice or evil. An action can be said to be unjust if it is out of alignment with a moral standard.[2]

A moral standard is commonly referred to as a law, which is why justice is equated with law-abidingness or lawfulness, and injustice with lawbreaking or lawlessness. For most of us, "law" brings to mind legal codes enacted by politicians and upheld by civil authorities. But justice isn't merely obeying man-made laws. In fact, sometimes justice demands that we *disobey* man-made laws. The Nazis had a law that forbade providing aid or shelter to Jews who were being rounded up and exterminated. If you obeyed that law, you were complicit in a horrific injustice.

This brings up an important question: How do we determine *which* man-made laws are just, and which are not? Is there a moral or legal standard that transcends man-made laws? Martin Luther King Jr. believed there was. America's most famous civil rights leader was arrested and jailed in 1963 for violating a court order forbidding him from protesting racial injustice in Birmingham, Alabama. In his famous *Letter from a Birmingham Jail* King wrote to fellow clergy who had criticized his "willingness to break laws."

> One may well ask, "How can you advocate breaking some laws and obeying others?" The answer is found in the fact that there are two types of laws: there are just laws, and there are unjust laws. I would agree with St. Augustine that "An unjust law is no law at all."
>
> Now, what is the difference between the two? How does one determine when a law is just or unjust? *A just law is a man-made code that squares with the moral law, or the law of God.* An unjust law is a code that is out of harmony with the moral law. To put it in the terms of St. Thomas Aquinas, an unjust law is a human law that is not rooted in eternal and natural law. [italics added][3]

King believed that a higher law exists—"the law of God." Christian apologist Greg Koukl calls this "the Law-over-everything-and-everyone."[4] So justice is conformity with this higher law. In this respect, justice is the same as truth. It requires a fixed point of reference that exists apart from man-made laws and our beliefs about what is good and right—a standard to which even the most powerful are accountable. Without this higher law, justice is arbitrary and changeable based on whoever wields power.

How do finite and fallible human beings discover this transcendent moral standard? We find it in God, the Creator of the universe, whose character is goodness, righteousness, and holiness (or moral perfection). As John Calvin said, the law reveals God's character.[5] *He* is the moral plumb line who determines what is good and right for all peoples, for all eras. And because God doesn't change, this standard doesn't change. God is the immovable "Rock" whose "work is perfect, for all his ways are justice. A God of faithfulness and without iniquity, just and upright is he" (Deuteronomy 32:4 ESV).

This excludes the Allah of Islam, who is ultimately unknowable. "Allah is a distant, remote being who reveals his will but not himself," says Daniel Janosik of Columbia International University. "It is impossible to know him in a personal way. In his absolute oneness there is unity but not trinity, and because of this lack of relationship, love is not emphasized."[6] Allah is not the personal, loving, and holy God of the Bible. Because the personal, triune God of Genesis 1:1 exists, and because His very character is good, the universe is both personal and moral. There is a true, eternal, and transcendent "good" that permeates the cosmos. And yet there is so much injustice! How do we uncover true justice in an unjust world? We go to God's Word, the unerring plumb line.

In the Bible, we translate the Hebrew words *tsedek* and *mishpat* as either "righteousness" or "justice," depending on the context. The Bible has more than thirty examples of "righteousness" and "justice" being used interchangeably. For example, "I walk in the way of righteousness, along the paths of justice" (Proverbs 8:20), or "The LORD works righteousness and justice for all the oppressed" (Psalm 103:6).[7] We see the similarity of these words, and their centrality to God's nature, in the vivid image of our great God who is "enthroned" as the King of Kings and Lord of Lords. He is the one true and righteous Judge. His justice, therefore, rooted in His character, is not strange.

The LORD reigns, let the earth be glad; let the distant shores rejoice. Clouds and thick darkness surround him; *righteousness and justice are the foundation of his throne.* (Psalm 97:1–2, italics added)

God is both righteous and just. If He were not righteous, He would not be just. If He were not just, He would not be righteous. Yet He is both! And He, not the changing consensus of elite opinion, is the plumb line by which we measure all claims of justice.

WHAT WE CANNOT *NOT* KNOW

I have asserted that God and His law provide the plumb line by which we can decide the merit of any claims of justice. But can we really know Him and His law? This question is urgent if we are to rightly respond to the moral chaos all around us (and in our own hearts).

We must acknowledge that such a transcendent moral standard exists, but it wouldn't be of any consequence if we had no knowledge of it. But God has made it known to us. How?

First, He communicates it to us *inwardly*. As image-bearers of God, all people have a built-in sense of this law "imprinted on our heart," so to speak. C. S. Lewis, in his classic work of apologetics, *Mere Christianity*, calls this innate moral code "a clue to the meaning of the universe." Lewis says that "human beings, all over the earth, have this curious idea that they ought to behave in a certain way, and cannot really get rid of it."[8]

The apostle Paul wrote about this in his epistle to the Romans: "When Gentiles, who do not have the law, do by nature things required by the law . . . they show that the requirements of *the law are written on their hearts*, their *consciences* also bearing witness, and their thoughts sometimes accusing them and at other times even defending them" (Romans 2:14–15, italics added). Natural law theory says that human beings can apprehend God's moral law through their God-given reason.[9]

Paul makes the audacious claim that *all people*—not only the Jews—know tacitly what God's eternal moral standard is, because they "do by nature things required by the law." They show that God has written it "on their hearts" because their consciences convict them of wrongdoing.

Consider for a moment how important this is. What would human relations be like if we didn't have an inward sense of right and wrong, a conscience, to guide us? What if none of us experienced guilt or shame for wrongdoing? We call someone who feels no remorse for wicked behavior a sociopath. John Wayne Gacy, Ted Bundy, and Jeffrey Dahmer were sociopaths. In a world filled with such people, evil would run amok. But in His grace, God provided a strong check against all this by writing His eternal moral code on our hearts. That is what justice does—it inhibits the spread of wickedness by establishing, affirming, and upholding what is good.

Second, when Paul says that gentiles (non-Jews) "do not have the law," he is referring to the *other* way God communicates His transcendent law to us, that is, through the Ten Commandments—the legal code handed down from God to humankind three and a half millennia ago. The Ten Commandments were "inscribed by the finger of God" (Exodus 31:18), delivered to Moses and the Jewish people, and through them, to all of us. This summary of God's moral law is one of His greatest gifts to humanity, because it provides the only true, unchanging foundation for justice in human history. This is why the image of the stone tablets is engraved at the apex of the United States Supreme Court building.

JUSTICE IN EVERYDAY LIFE

Justice means a lot more than checking off a list of rules, of course. It means living in right relationship with others—with God, and with human beings made in His image. It defines how we *ought* to treat others—what kind of behavior is good and right, and what is not. As Micah 6:8 says:

> He has told you, O man, what is good;
>> and what does the Lord require of you
> but to do justice, and to love kindness,
>> and to walk humbly with your God? (ESV)

Gary Breshears, a theology professor at Western Seminary in Portland, Oregon, explains what the Hebrew word *tsedek* (translated into English as "justice") means: "a life in which all relationships—human to human, human to God, and human to creation—are well-ordered and harmonious."[10] Justice, in this sense, is similar to *shalom*, the deep peace and harmony that result from relationships in alignment with God's perfect moral standard.

Practically, justice means "following the rule of law, showing impartiality, paying what you promised, not stealing, not swindling, not taking bribes, and not taking advantage of the weak because they are too uninformed or unconnected to stop you," according to pastor Kevin DeYoung.[11]

This kind of everyday justice was the central message that John the Baptist preached to the crowds on the banks of the Jordan River. He warned the people of God's coming judgment. In response, the people asked what they could do to avoid God's wrath. John replied this way: "Anyone who has two shirts should share with the one who has none, and anyone who has food should do the same" (Luke 3:11). When tax collectors asked the same question, John responded: "Don't collect any more [tax] than you are required to" (Luke 3:13). When soldiers inquired of him, he replied: "Don't extort money and don't accuse people falsely—be content with your pay" (Luke 3:14).

In short, justice is living out the Ten Commandments in our everyday relationships.

"We do justice when we give all human beings their due as creations of God," Tim Keller says,[12] paraphrasing Aristotle. The last part of this sentence is key: "as creations of God." Justice requires recognizing what it means to be human—that we all possess inherent dignity and worth, with (in the Declaration's immortal phrasing) "unalienable rights."[13] To "do justice" is to treat others as uniquely valuable, and to respect their God-given rights. It is "loving your neighbor as yourself."[14] This is sometimes called *communitive justice*, and it is the duty of every human being.

JUSTICE AS FAIR, IMPARTIAL JUDGMENT

But there is another kind of justice. *Distributive justice* is reserved for God-ordained authorities—including parents in the home, pastors in the church, and civil authorities in the state. Distributive justice demands that authorities render judgments fairly, treating everyone equally before the law, because that is how God—the supreme authority in the universe—treats us. He impartially rewards good and punishes evil. He does not ignore the sins of any. He does not take bribes (Deuteronomy 10:17).

Justice demands that injustice be punished. If evil goes unpunished, injustice multiplies. "Justice means exacting an appropriate payment for a crime," Koukl says. "No payment, no justice."[15] We commonly say that lawbreakers must be held "to account" for their crimes, bringing to mind accounting concepts such as debts, payments, and balance sheets. Proper accounting requires that the books be balanced. So does justice.

An ancient (and still common) image that represents justice is a blindfolded woman with balanced scales in her hand. The blindfold represents the impartiality before the law that a just decision requires. The scales represent the balance that justice demands. Those who commit injustice incur a *debt* against their victims, and the scale is out of balance. That debt may be stolen property, or freedom, or innocence, or reputation, or even life. Justice demands that balance be restored—the debt has to be paid.

> **Justice:** Conformity to God's moral standard, particularly as revealed in the Ten Commandments and the royal law: "Love your neighbor as yourself" (James 2:8). There are two kinds of justice. (1) *Communitive justice* is living in right relationship with God and with others. Giving people their due as image-bearers of God. (2) *Distributive justice* is impartially rendering judgment, righting wrongs, and meting out punishment for lawbreaking. Distributive justice is reserved for God and God-ordained authorities, including parents in the home, pastors in the church, and civil authorities in the state.

Authorities must carefully search for the truth to justly render a judgment. Claims of wrongdoing have to be backed up with corroborating evidence, truthfully presented. Witnesses must offer accurate testimony. Perjury is a grievous injustice, a violation the ninth commandment, "You shall not bear false witness against your neighbor" (Exodus 20:16 ESV). In other words, *justice requires truth*. In the words of Christian apologist Ravi Zacharias, "Justice is the handmaiden of truth, and when truth dies, justice is buried with it."[16]

INJUSTICE AND THE FALL

If justice means treating others in conformity with God's perfect moral standard, then we must admit that *injustice* is pervasive in our fallen world. Yes, we possess a conscience to guide us in right behavior. But as fallen creatures, we also possess a built-in inclination to break the law. In our fallen nature, we want to be *autonomous*—a law unto ourselves. Given the right circumstances, we find it all too easy to shade the truth, cheat, steal, slander, abuse, attack, or worse—all for selfish ends. On top of this, we need no special training to justify bad behavior. It comes naturally to blame others. Not only do we regularly treat other people in ways that we should not, but more significantly, we do the same with God. We ignore and reject the One who created and sustains us, replacing Him with the idols of money, success, approval, sex, or comfort.

Because of our fallen nature, we are double-minded when it comes to justice. We cry out for justice when we, our friends, or our loved ones have been mistreated, but we find it inconvenient when we are doing the mistreating. We make excuses for our bad behavior, or we brush it aside, saying it isn't that serious. We claim our innocence in the face of all evidence. Once, after visiting a prison, the evangelist D. L. Moody quipped, "Why, I never saw so many innocent men together in my life."[17]

Look again at the Ten Commandments (and Jesus's amplification of them in the Sermon on the Mount).[18] Are you sure you measure up to God's perfect standard of justice? Here are some questions that Gregory Koukl encourages each of us to ponder:

- Have you ever placed anything before or above God in your life?
- Have you ever disobeyed or dishonored your parents?
- Have you ever deceived anyone or misrepresented the truth in any way?
- Have you ever taken something that was not yours?
- Have you ever been sexually intimate with someone who was not, at the time, your spouse?
- Have you ever toyed with the idea in your mind?[19]

There is simply no denying it. By the only standard that ultimately matters, we are all guilty of injustice. We are all lawbreakers. "The evil in the world is not out there," says Koukl. "It is in us. Put simply, we are guilty, and we know it."[20]

It gets worse. We've not merely wronged other people. We've wronged God Himself. We have *sinned*. To sin is to violate God's law. Because God is the ultimate standard for goodness, He is ultimately the offended party. "Against you, and you only, have I sinned and done what is evil in your sight, so that you are right in your verdict and justified when you judge," said King David in Psalm 51:4. David was guilty of the vilest evil, using his power to commit adultery with Bathsheba and attempting to cover it up by murdering her husband, Uriah. But David recognized that, ultimately, he had sinned against God by flouting His eternal standard of righteousness. Likely, your transgressions don't rise to the level of David's, but that doesn't let you off the hook.

None is righteous, no, not one; . . . all have sinned and
fall short of the glory of God. (Romans 3:9, 23 ESV)

God isn't indifferent to injustice. It is abhorrent to Him. "For
the wrath of God is revealed from heaven against all ungodliness
and unrighteousness of men" (Romans 1:18). Today Christians
are uncomfortable talking about God's wrath. We prefer to dwell
on His love, mercy, and forgiveness. Those are all wonderfully
true, but if we fail to reckon with God's hatred of injustice, our
picture of Him is incomplete, even false. Because of his moral
goodness, God cannot abide injustice. And would you really
want Him to? He wouldn't be good if He overlooked evil. Rather,
He'd be complicit in it, and this will *never* be true of God. His
own holy nature, the source of all justice, prevents it.

God's compassion stirs in Him a hatred for injustice. He
is tenderhearted toward its victims. He sees their tears, storing
them in a bottle (Psalm 56:8).

He will deliver the needy who cry out, the afflicted
who have no one to help. He will take pity on the
weak and the needy and save the needy from death.
He will rescue them from oppression and violence, for
precious is their blood in his sight. (Psalm 72:12–14)

God rises up in anger against those who oppress the weak,
the marginalized, and the poor. He will hold every oppressor
accountable.

God is fully committed to dealing with evil and injustice.
No injustice will be overlooked—not yours, mine, or anyone
else's. Every lawless act will be accounted for. The Bible, from
Genesis 3 to Revelation, tells the sweeping drama of God's history-

encompassing plan to restore justice to a fallen world rife with injustice and evil. But there is good news. God provides a way of escaping the punishment and wrath that our rebellion has earned us—a way that displays God's glory in all its radiant splendor.

THE GREAT DILEMMA

God's justice is tied, like all of His attributes, to His goodness or righteousness. But His goodness shows itself in other qualities as well, such as His love and mercy. These qualities come together in one of the most important passages of Scripture: Exodus 34:6–7, the account of God appearing to Moses on Mount Sinai and proclaiming His name. "The LORD passed before [Moses] and proclaimed,

> The LORD, the LORD, a God merciful and gracious,
> slow to anger, and abounding in steadfast love and
> faithfulness, keeping steadfast love for thousands,
> forgiving iniquity and transgression and sin, but who
> will by no means clear the guilty, visiting the iniquity of
> the fathers on the children and the children's children,
> to the third and the fourth generation. (ESV)

Notice how love, mercy, and justice are central to God's character. He is "merciful, gracious, abounding in steadfast love." And yet He "will by no means clear the guilty." This presents a seeming dilemma, for mercy is the act of withholding justly deserved punishment.

What if God were just but not merciful? Would He still be good? No. He'd be like the infamous Inspector Javert in Victor Hugo's *Les Miserables*, a man ruthlessly committed to justice, yet without a shred of mercy. And yet, what if He were merciful but not just? If God overlooked evil, He would likewise not be good. Such a God would be culpable in the proliferation of evil. God is merciful *and* just, and we who seek justice but who require mercy ought to be glad. In the wonderful words of Psalm 85:10, "Love and faithfulness meet together; righteousness and peace kiss each other." What real-life model presents this great juxtaposition?

We find it at the apex of God's extraordinary story of redemption—the life, death, and resurrection of Jesus Christ. God incarnate, in an act of sheer love, took upon Himself the punishment we deserved for our transgressions in order to show us a mercy we could never deserve. The New Testament writers expressed their wonder at this over and over again:

> There is no difference between Jew and Gentile, for all have sinned and fall short of the glory of God, and all are justified freely by his grace through the redemption that came by Christ Jesus. God presented Christ as a sacrifice of atonement, through the shedding of his blood—to be received by faith. He did this to demonstrate his righteousness . . . *so as to be just and the one who justifies those who have faith in Jesus."* (Romans 3:22–26, italics added)

> "God made him who had no sin to be sin for us, so that in him we might become the righteousness of God. (2 Corinthians 5:21)

> "For Christ also died for sins once for all, the just for the unjust, so that He might bring us to God." (1 Peter 3:18 NASB)

Perhaps the clearest picture of the great transaction was recorded by the prophet Isaiah some seven hundred years before the birth of Jesus:

> Surely he took up our pain
> > and bore our suffering,
> yet we considered him punished by God,
> > stricken by him, and afflicted.
> But he was pierced for our transgressions,
> > he was crushed for our iniquities;
> the punishment that brought us peace was on him,
> > and by his wounds we are healed.
> We all, like sheep, have gone astray,
> > each of us has turned to our own way;
> and the Lord has laid on him
> > the iniquity of us all. (Isaiah 53:4–6)

This is the good news at the heart of the biblical redemption story. God's mercy and justice meet at the cross. This indescribable gift of forgiveness in Jesus Christ is available to all, no matter how great our sins.

Tragically, many will reject this gift. Some will reject Jesus, refusing to believe He was who He said. Some will reject God as a superstitious fairy tale, denying the existence of an objective, transcendent moral law. Others will prefer to "earn" their salvation, thinking their good deeds will merit God's favor. But it doesn't work this way. Every thought, word, or act that violates God's perfect moral standard incurs a debt, and that debt has to be paid. If we reject the payment Christ made on our behalf, then we will have to pay it ourselves. One way or the other, a price has to be paid, for in the end, perfect justice will prevail.

JUSTICE AND MERCY IN THE SHADOW OF THE CROSS

The cross is God's ultimate solution for dealing with the evil and injustice in this world. Calvary made achieving this goal possible, but it won't happen fully until Jesus returns. God delays the final judgment for the moment, knowing full well that evil and injustice will continue. He delays it, not because He is powerless over evil nor because He lacks compassion for its victims. He delays it for the sake of mercy, for God is "patient . . . not wanting anyone to perish, but everyone to come to repentance" (2 Peter 3:9).

But His patience won't last forever. When Jesus returns, He will be the Judge. On that day, perfect justice will be done. Evil will be punished, wounds will be mended, tears will be wiped away, and the world will be made right again.[21]

> Then I saw a great white throne and him who was seated on it. The earth and the heavens fled from his presence, and there was no place for them. And I saw the dead, great and small, standing before the throne, and books were opened. Another book was opened, which is the book of life. The dead were judged according to what they had done as recorded in the books. . . . each person was judged according to what they had done. . . . Anyone whose name was not found written in the book of life was thrown into the lake of fire. (Revelation 20:11–13, 15)

All will stand before this judgment seat, and books will be opened. One will contain a record of everything we've ever done. Every one of our thoughts and actions will be judged against God's perfect moral standard. Nothing will be hidden. There will be no escaping justice.

But mercifully, there is another book—the Book of Life. It too contains a record. It lists the names of those who, though guilty, have received mercy simply by requesting it. How? The punishment for their lawbreaking was paid for on the cross. In this judgment on the last day, it won't matter if you are male or female, black or white, rich or poor. The only divide that will matter will be the one between the "poor in spirit" who cry out for mercy, and the proud who do not.

As surely as the sun rises, that day will come. But until then, the church has work to do. We are to let the world know that mercy and forgiveness are available through the finished work of Christ. We are to give our neighbors a foretaste of the coming kingdom by modeling justice in our relationships and in fighting injustice wherever it appears. We will examine that kingdom work in the next chapter.

CHAPTER 3

JUSTICE BEFORE THE JUDGMENT

A s a teenage gymnast on the US Olympic team, Rachael Denhollander was sexually assaulted repeatedly by team doctor Larry Nassar—a serial abuser with over 260 young female victims. In 2016, she filed a police complaint that ultimately led to Nassar's conviction and a prison sentence of 40 to 175 years.

During the trial, the judge gave Denhollander permission to speak directly to Nassar. Her testimony revealed a deep wisdom about justice and mercy in the shadow of the cross. This courageous Christian wife, mother, and attorney spoke of the terrible evil Nassar committed: "You have become a man ruled by selfish and perverted desires. . . . You chose to pursue your wickedness no matter what it cost others." She reminded Nassar that in addition to earthly judgment, he would face a future heavenly judgment in which "all of God's wrath and eternal terror is poured out on men like you."[1]

Yet justice isn't the whole story. There is also mercy, and that is where Denhollander turned next: "Should you ever reach the point of truly facing what you have done, the guilt will be crushing. And that is what makes the gospel of Christ so sweet, because it extends grace and hope and mercy where none should be found. And it will be there for you."

Then Denhollander did something miraculous. She offered Nassar her forgiveness. "I pray you experience the soul crushing weight of guilt, so you may someday experience true repentance and true forgiveness from God, which you need far more than forgiveness from me—though I extend that to you as well."

In committing this horrific injustice, Nassar incurred a debt against Denhollander and his other victims. He also incurred a debt against God for breaking His eternal moral standard. For justice to prevail, that debt has to be paid. Partial justice was served through the earthly court in Michigan on January 24, 2018, but perfect justice will be served if a forgiven Nassar is ushered into God's heavenly throne room, his sins paid for by Christ's perfect sacrifice.

If, however, Nassar hardens his heart and dies without Christ, he will face God's wrath. In the words of the apostle Paul, "Because of [his] stubbornness and [his] unrepentant heart, [he is] storing up wrath against [himself] for the day of God's wrath, when [God's] righteous judgment will be revealed" (Romans 2:5). But as Denhollander blessedly reminds us, if Nassar is remorseful and repents, God will (paraphrasing Colossians 2:14) "cancel the charge of his legal indebtedness, which stands against him and condemns him, *taking it away by nailing it to the cross*." He won't deserve this in any way. It is a gift. *It is amazing grace.*

Because of the cross, Denhollander forgave Nassar. To forgive someone who has inflicted such trauma is, humanly speaking, impossible. But with God, all things are possible

(Matthew 19:26). Denhollander can forgive because she knows that she has been forgiven, and she too is unworthy of God's mercy. She forgives, knowing that a future reckoning is coming, leaving the dispensing of justice in God's capable hands.

As the apostle Paul exhorts in Romans 12:19 (ESV), "Beloved, never avenge yourselves, but leave it to the wrath of God, for it is written, 'Vengeance is mine, I will repay, says the Lord.'" It is not our job to root out all of earth's evil. Rather, we are called to love our neighbors and enemies alike, knowing that God will deal with evil decisively when He returns.

What does this kind of love look like? Romans 12:20–21 (ESV) provides helpful insights.

> "If your enemy is hungry, feed him; if he is thirsty, give him something to drink; for by so doing you will heap burning coals on his head." Do not be overcome by evil, but overcome evil with good.

Pastor John Piper believes that this means we are not to let an enemy's hostility produce hostility in us. Piper says, "Don't be overcome by *his* evil. Don't let another person's evil make you evil."[2] Because of the cross, Denhollander is overcoming evil with good with a man who hurt her and so many others.

In a world teeming with injustices large and small, the cross of Christ encourages us to overcome evil with good while we await God's perfect justice at the final judgment, when all the scales will be put in perfect balance. In the meantime, we are called to work for justice and mercy in our daily lives and in the world.

A CULTURE BUILT ON JUSTICE AND MERCY

"Justice, sir, is the great interest of [people] on earth," said Daniel Webster. "It is the ligament which holds civilized beings and civilized nations together."[3] Webster was right. Without justice, human flourishing is impossible.

Those of us who grew up in cultures profoundly shaped by a Judeo-Christian worldview often fail to appreciate the unique inheritance of our relatively just societies. We take for granted that human beings have inalienable rights and deserve respect, and that those accused of wrongdoing are entitled to due process. We forget that in the broad sweep of history, relatively just societies are the exception, not the rule.

On this side of Christ's return, there will be no perfectly just societies, yet some will be more just than others. What are some of the hallmarks that set these societies apart?

Acknowledgment of a transcendent lawgiver

Just societies acknowledge a moral law higher than themselves and a supreme lawgiver to whom even the most powerful are accountable. America's founders acknowledged both in the first sentence of the Declaration of Independence:

> When in the Course of human events it becomes necessary for one people to dissolve the political bands which have connected them with another and to assume among the powers of the earth, the separate and equal station to which *the Laws of Nature and of Nature's God* entitle them, a decent respect to the opinions of mankind requires that they should declare the causes which impel them to the separation. [italics added]

This was intentional. Unless justice is founded upon a transcendent, objective basis of righteousness, it necessarily will be founded on man-made morality, imposed by whoever holds power.

Respect for the rule of law

Just societies are built upon the rule of law, the understanding that the law applies equally to everyone. The rule of law says that those who create laws and administer justice are under, and must themselves adhere to, the law. They are not free to change or adapt the law to produce a preferred outcome that favors their interests or harms their opponents. Unjust societies, by contrast, are governed by the rule of man, which acknowledges no transcendent law.

Human dignity and God-granted human rights

Just societies are built upon the truth that all human beings are God's image-bearers and, as such, have equal dignity, incalculable worth, and rights that cannot be taken away. "All men are created equal, [and] . . . are endowed by their Creator with certain unalienable Rights." Just societies agree with C. S. Lewis, who wrote, "There are no ordinary people. You have never talked to a mere mortal. . . . Next to the Blessed Sacrament itself, your neighbour is the holiest object presented to your senses."[4]

Sarah Irving-Stonebraker grew up in Australia as a well-meaning but thoroughgoing secularist who had never examined the implications of her worldview. That began to change after she attended three lectures at Oxford University by the atheist philosopher Peter Singer. Irving-Stonebraker realized that atheism provided no rationale for human worth and equality.

I remember leaving Singer's lectures with a strange intellectual vertigo; I was committed to believing that universal human value was more than just a well-meaning conceit of liberalism. But I knew from my own research in the history of European empires and their encounters with indigenous cultures, that societies have always had different conceptions of human worth, or lack thereof. The premise of human equality is not a self-evident truth: it is profoundly historically contingent. I began to realize that the implications of my atheism were incompatible with almost every value I held dear.[5]

As Irving-Stonebraker realized, atheism has no basis for human dignity, and without human dignity and equality, there is no justice. This is why just societies maintain a high view of all human life. Just societies uphold the inherent dignity of all people, regardless of sex, skin color, sexual behavior, ethnicity, or religion, from conception to natural death.

Injustice results when certain groups are dehumanized. In early America, slaves were viewed as less than fully human by many. Today, the unborn are as well. To the extent that racism and anti-Semitism continue, so are African Americans and Jewish people.

Ideological social justice is based on the belief that evil and injustice are the products of dominant groups who create systems and structures which marginalize others and promote their own interests. Ironically, this belief can be used to marginalized and dehumanize people who find themselves in a dominant cultural group, such as men, whites, and heterosexuals. Consider the case of the *New York Times* hiring Sarah Jeong to be an editorial writer despite her history of writing racist, antiwhite tweets.[6] When human beings are treated as less than human, unspeakable evil results.

A check on corruption

One of the greatest blights on any nation is corruption—the abuse of power for personal (usually financial) gain. Transparency International's Corruption Perceptions Index[7] reveals that, with few exceptions, the countries with the lowest levels of corruption were born out of a Judeo-Christian framework. Those without this advantage tend to have higher perceived levels of public sector corruption, according to experts and businesspeople.

The reason is straightforward. Societies are built in the image of the God, or gods, that they collectively worship. If the gods are selfish, capricious, and unpredictable—if they can be bribed for special treatment—then the culture will follow along with high levels of bribery and corruption. But if the culture is shaped and formed by the worship of the true, living God who "love[s] righteousness and hate[s] wickedness" (Psalm 45:7) and "is not partial, and takes no bribes" (Deuteronomy 10:17 ESV), corruption will be significantly checked.

A Kenyan pastor speaking with my colleague Darrow Miller had an "ah-ha!" moment along these lines, asking, "So, you are telling me that giving a bribe is an act of worship?" "Yes," replied Darrow. "But not an act of worship to the living God. If you give a bribe, you must confess that you are not worshiping the living God, but a pagan god." Then the lights went on: "So doing justice is an act of worship of the living God." "Yes," replied Darrow. "That is exactly right."

Establishing due process

Due process is called *due* process because it describes the kind of respectful treatment that the accused are due as image-bearers of God. It entails certain definable elements that are applied impartially. These include: (1) the right to a timely trial by an unbiased judge and jury; (2) the presumption of innocence until guilt has been established by the testimony of multiple witnesses, and the presentation of corroborating evidence; (3) the right of the accused to be informed of the charges against him or her; (4) the right of the accused to confront his or her accusers, and to cross-examine opposing witnesses; (5) the right of the accused to be represented by legal counsel; and (6) the right of the accused to defend himself or herself, including the calling of witnesses.[8]

Due process is another fruit of Judeo-Christian civilization. Its biblical roots go back to passages such as Deuteronomy 19:15, which says, "One witness is not enough to convict anyone accused of any crime or offense they may have committed. A matter must be established by the testimony of two or three witnesses." Likewise, in the New Testament, God is described as one who "judges each person's work impartially" (1 Peter 1:17). Therefore, earthly judges should be fair and impartial, for their authority to judge comes from God (Romans 13:1). These principles have been passed down, generation by generation, and were encoded in the Magna Carta and the US Constitution. Just societies value, protect, and preserve due process.

Entrusting final judgment to God

Just societies understand that not every wrong will be righted on this side of Christ's return. They remember that ultimate justice is to be dispensed thoroughly and perfectly by God's Son, Jesus Christ (John 5:22), and that a day of final accounting is coming. As Paul proclaimed atop the Areopagus to the pagan philosophers of ancient Rome:

> "The times of ignorance God overlooked, but now he commands all people everywhere to repent, because he has fixed a day on which he will judge the world in righteousness by a man whom he has appointed; and of this he has given assurance to all by raising him from the dead" (Acts 17:30–31).

By not forcing this future judgment into the present, Christians have the space to extend grace and mercy in the face of the world's evil, even as they try to redress injustice when possible. While church history, tragically, is dotted with horrible episodes of inquisition or crusade by men who foolishly sought to take God's judgment into their own hands, the main trajectory of Judeo-Christian faith has produced civilizations that uphold the principles of justice and are able to critique—and often correct—violations of that justice.

This is not the case with those who deny God and the final judgment, who dismiss religion as the "opiate of the masses." Believing in no ultimate Judge who will separate the sheep from the goats, they take it upon themselves to mete out perfect justice. They believe that every moral grievance must be immediately redressed until we have perfected society. The tens of millions of people starved to death, executed, imprisoned, and aborted under communism testify to the harsh reality of this kind of human judgment. Such utopian visions have no basis for grace or mercy.

Despite the well-known track record of horrors produced by this kind of godless mindset, we are seeing it return in the form of a redefined "justice" that goes by the name "social justice." As we will see, it isn't just at all.

CHAPTER 4

JUSTICE REDEFINED

A perfectly holy and righteous Creator has woven justice deeply into the cosmos, and our hearts know it. When seemingly senseless tragedy strikes, a Christian will naturally ask, "Why?" . . . and even an atheist will rage against God.

Even if we deny God's existence, we cannot live as if justice does not exist. We cannot accept a universe that is uncaring or indifferent to evil. Rather, if we deny God, we will create our own codes of morality, our own standards of justice. If we abandon a transcendent plumb line to distinguish between good and evil, our only alternative is to accept a man-made standard. Of course, any such standard will be changeable, arbitrary, and beholden to the whims of those who wield power.

> **Justice Redefined:** The tearing down of traditional structures and systems deemed to be oppressive, and the redistribution of power and resources from oppressors to victims in pursuit of equality of outcome.

Today, an ideology (and accompanying movement) described by its adherents as "social justice" has radically redefined the popular understanding of justice. In contrast to the older understanding of justice based on Judeo-Christian revelation, this new ideology is characterized by its:

- obsession with power, oppression, and victimization— It sees a world divided between evil oppressors and innocent victims in a zero-sum power struggle; nothing exists outside these categories.
- use of tactics reminiscent of Mao's Cultural Revolution and an "ends justifies the means" methodology
- fixation on class, race, gender, and sexual orientation as defining characteristics of personal identity— Individuals are "nondescript representatives of their taxonomic class."[1]
- hostility toward Judeo-Christian religion, particularly in its beliefs about family and sexuality
- antipathy toward the natural family, and specifically the authority of parents with their children, and the authority of the husband in the home
- fixation on redistributing wealth and power by an ever-larger state

This hugely influential ideology is deadly serious. It is nothing less than a kind of cultural acid, eating away at the central pillars of a free, just, and open society. We dismiss it at our peril.

SHIFTING WORLDVIEWS

To understand how social justice ideology has displaced biblical understandings of justice, we first must explore two momentous worldview shifts in the West beginning in the early eighteenth century. At the core of any culture is a "cult," a deeply held religious belief system. A worldview shift involves replacing one "cult," one morality, and one system of justice with another.

The first shift happened during the Enlightenment when the worldview I'll call premodernism was displaced by modernism. Premodern belief systems acknowledge a spiritual reality that transcends the universe. Though they are highly complex and sophisticated systems of belief that have built enduring civilizations, the great monotheistic religions—Judaism, Christianity, and Islam—are all premodern. Ultimate authority is vested in God and in His revealed will. Modernism, however, dispensed with God and the spiritual realm, defining reality in material terms alone. For modern man, science is the final arbiter of truth.

Then, starting in the mid-1900s, modernism began to give way to postmodernism. Postmodernism grounds reality, not in God or in the material universe, but in man himself—in the sovereign, autonomous individual. "Truth" is now internal, personal, and subjective—a product of human imagination. Where modernism left us with a purposeless world of matter in motion, the postmodern prophet Friedrich Nietzsche posited the Übermensch, the super man, who would courageously impose his will on reality.

Three Momentous Shifts in Western Worldviews[2]

Worldview	Dates	Reality	Supreme Authority
Premodern	Prior to the 17th century	Spiritual and material	God and His Word (e.g., the Ten Commandments)
Modernism	18th to 20th centuries	Material only	Science
Postmodernism	20th century to present	The human mind	The autonomous, sovereign self

Postmodernism views human beings as autonomous, self-determining agents. The word "autonomous" is derived from two Greek words, *autos*, meaning "self," and *nomos*, meaning "law." To be autonomous is to be a law unto oneself. Gone is any notion of a transcendent, objective moral law, or even the natural laws of modernity. Reality is now subjective, the product of human minds.

Because postmodernism sees all reality as subjective, we no longer have a basis for human rights. Life and liberty have been replaced by a new overarching human right: "The right to define one's own concept of existence, of meaning, of the universe, and of the mystery of human life," as famously expressed by Supreme Court Justice Anthony Kennedy.[3] Postmodern man is the source and definer of reality.

SOCIAL CHAOS

But there's an obvious problem. If each person is a law unto himself or herself, on what basis can a society be ordered? Who has ultimate authority when we are our own little gods? Postmodernism's grounding of reality in the autonomous, sovereign individual turns out to be unworkable. It leads to social chaos—with every idea (except Judeo-Christian theism) accorded a place of honor in the public square, with people no longer sure of their own sex, with vicious hatreds writ large on social media, in the streets, and in politics, with irreconcilable differences being the norm.

For millennia, the Judeo-Christian worldview gave the West an overarching narrative, a framework and basis for justice, and sufficient grounding for human dignity. Today, all this has been cast aside, as that which formerly brought order to society and meaning and purpose to the individual has been abandoned.

The worldview vacuum did not last long, of course. German social theorist Karl Marx (1818–1883) created a new narrative, *a new worldview*—a new religion, in fact—to replace the Judeo-Christian worldview as the West's new "cult."

Marx's religion is based on modern, atheistic assumptions but is nonetheless compatible with postmodern thought categories, allowing these two worldviews to coexist quite happily in the post-Christian West. Both postmodernism and Marxism trace their lineage back to European Romanticism and Idealism, to philosophers such as Kant, Hegel, and Nietzsche. Not surprisingly, the most influential postmodern theorists, Michel Foucault (1926–1984) and Jacques Derrida (1930–2004), were greatly influenced by Marxism, with Foucault serving for a time as a member of the French Communist Party.[4]

Throughout the twentieth century, Marx's religious metanarrative was put to the test, first in Russia under Lenin and Stalin, then in China under Mao, and later in North Korea, Vietnam, Cambodia, and Cuba. These vast social experiments were unmitigated disasters, producing prison states, gulags, and genocides that killed hundreds of millions.

And yet despite this miserable track record, Marxism remains with us. Although in a different guise, Marx's deadly theory, incredibly, has become the most influential worldview in the West. As communist states were beginning to collapse in the mid-twentieth century, a new generation of Marxist theorists arose in Europe to rescue the movement. These included Antonio Gramsci (1891–1937), Herbert Marcuse (1898–1979), and Max Horkheimer (1895–1973). Their informal network became known as the Frankfurt School,[5] and their reboot of Marxism (sometimes referred to as "neo-Marxism" or "cultural Marxism") was incubated in universities in the United States and Europe under the broad heading of "critical social theory."

Marx's worldview is built on the notion that the world can be divided into two basic categories: evil oppressors and innocent victims. Oppressors exercise their power and domination (their "hegemony," according to Gramsci) through establishing and maintaining a network of often stealthy social institutions, structures, and systems that result in their being advantaged (or "privileged" in common parlance) in a host of ways. Marx limited his focus to the structures and systems that resulted in *economic inequality* between *classes*.

Marxism 1.0

Good	Evil	
Oppressed victims (morally innocent)	Oppressive systems and structures	Oppressors (morally guilty)
The working class (the proletariat)	Capitalism	Wealthy property owners and capitalists (the bourgeoisie)

The Frankfurt School social theorists expanded Marx's economic, class-based framework to include inequalities between other groups, including ethnic groups, the sexes, and gender identity groups (LGBTQ+). The result is the same. As Nancy Pearcey explains, "Just as in classic Marxism, the proposed solution is to raise your consciousness (become aware of yourself as an oppressed group), then rise up against the oppressor."[6]

Marxism 2.0 (Cultural Marxism or Social Justice)[7]

Good	Evil	
Oppressed victims (morally innocent)	Oppressive systems and structures	Oppressors (morally guilty)
Class—The working class (the proletariat)	Capitalism	Property owners (the bourgeoisie)
Race—Ethnic minorities (people of color)	White supremacy ("whiteness")	Whites
Sex—Females	The patriarchy	Males
Gender—LGBTQ+	Judeo-Christian morality	Orthodox Christians, Jews, and other sexual traditionalists

By utilizing a cultural strategy that some have called "the long march through the institutions,"[8] the Frankfurt School social theorists and their allies achieved stunning success at embedding their presuppositions into Western public education, academia, the media, entertainment, big business, and politics. Today, ideological social justice dominates the commanding heights of Western culture, and has even made significant inroads into mainstream evangelicalism.

"History repeats itself," Karl Marx reportedly stated, "first as tragedy, second as farce." Here's just one example of how Karl Marx's theory is repeating itself courtesy of radical feminist Shulamith Firestone, who as early as the 1970s began to apply the neo-Marxist framework to male-female relationships:

So that just as to assure elimination of economic classes requires the revolt of the underclass (the proletariat) and, in a temporary dictatorship, their seizure of the means of *production*, so to assure the elimination of sexual classes requires the revolt of the underclass (women) and the seizure of control of *reproduction*: not only the full restoration to women of ownership of their own bodies, but also their (temporary) seizure of control of human fertility—the new population biology as well as all the social institutions of child-bearing and child-rearing. And just as the end goal of socialist revolution was not only the elimination of the economic class *privilege* but of the economic class *distinction* itself, so the end goal of feminist revolution must be, unlike that of the first feminist movement, not just the elimination of male privilege but of the sex *distinction* itself: genital differences between human beings would no longer matter culturally.[9]

What's to account for the wild success of Marxism 2.0 in Western culture? While secularism severely undermined Christianity in Europe and the Americas, it couldn't provide a compelling religious alternative to fill the vacuum and meet the innate human need for morality and purpose. Ideological social justice is perhaps best understood as a postmodern religious alternative (a "successor ideology") to Christianity. Essayist Andrew Sullivan explains its appeal:

> For many, especially the young, discovering a new meaning [for life] . . . is thrilling. Social justice ideology does everything a religion should. It offers an account of the whole: that human life and society . . . must be seen entirely as a function of social power structures, in which various groups have spent all human existence oppressing other groups, and it provides a

set of principles to resist and reverse this interlocking web of oppression.[10]

Many people have decided that fighting for social justice is the new purpose for their lives.

THE POWER OF WORLDVIEWS

Before unpacking ideological social justice further, it will help to briefly explain what worldviews are and why they matter so much.

A worldview "is the [mental] window by which we view the world, and decide, often subconsciously, what is real and important, or unreal and unimportant"[11] says Phillip Johnson in his foreword to Nancy Pearcey's powerful book, *Total Truth*. Dallas Willard similarly writes: Our "worldview . . . consists of the most general and basic assumptions about what is real and what is good—including our assumptions about who we are and what we should do."[12] These "general and basic assumptions" come to each of us from our surrounding culture. We pick them up from our family, teachers, friends, and ultimately from the broader culture through films, television, and social media.

As social beings, we are profoundly shaped by our surrounding culture. Every one of us has a worldview. Nobody can "opt out." Willard goes on to explain that our worldviews "lie outside our consciousness . . . embedded in our body and in its social environment, including our history, language and culture. [Our worldviews] radiate throughout our life as background assumptions." Johnson concurs: "Our worldview governs our thinking even when—or especially when—we are unaware of it."

The word "govern" is very important here. Your worldview is not simply a set of ideas floating through your head, with no bearing on the rest of your life. Rather, it determines how you behave—how you function within your family, in your workplace, and in the broader community. It determines the type of society you create with others. Willard says that "there is nothing more practical than our worldview, for it determines the orientation of everything else we think and do. . . . What we assume to be real and what we assume to be valuable will govern our attitudes and actions. Period."

Because worldviews are comprised of background assumptions, many of which we are not consciously aware of, it is sometimes tricky to know what our worldview is. However, worldviews are discerned, over time, by our actions, the choices we make, and how we live. Our worldviews are proven by our actions more than our words. You can think of a worldview like the roots of a fruit tree. You cannot see the roots. They exist below the surface. Yet they determine the kind of fruit the tree will produce, and the fruit *can* be seen. Jesus said, "By their fruit you will recognize them" (Matthew 7:15–20).

Objective truth is recorded in the pages of Scripture, revealed in creation, and known, in part, through the proper use of human reason and logic. Yet Jesus warns us that lies also exist, and often they are subtle and difficult to detect. They arrive through "false prophets," who "come to you in sheep's clothing, but inwardly they are ferocious wolves" (Matthew 7:15).

As followers of Jesus Christ, the apostle Paul exhorts us to be attuned to these lies and false cultural presuppositions: "See to it that no one takes you captive through hollow and deceptive philosophy, which depends on human tradition and the elemental spiritual forces of this world rather than on Christ" (Colossians 2:8). We must no longer "conform to the pattern of this world, but be transformed by the renewing of [our] mind" (Romans 12:2). In short, we are called to think and act differently—not in accord with the accepted norms, attitudes, and behaviors of our surrounding culture, but in accordance with reality as presented in God's Word.

This exchange of false worldview presuppositions for true, biblical ones does not happen automatically when we receive Christ as Savior. It is a lifelong process, and it isn't easy or simple. We must be intentional about uncovering unconsciously held assumptions, exposing them to the light of Scripture. In other words, we must determine to "take captive every thought to make it obedient to Christ" (2 Corinthians 10:5).

This is a discipline. We have to develop the habit and practice of thinking "worldviewishly." But we are not without powerful help in this endeavor. God provides all that we need to be successful. He fills us with His Holy Spirit—the Spirit of Truth who guides us into all truth (John 16:13). He gives us His precious and divinely powerful Word that reveals truth to us, and serves as a lamp to our feet and a light to our path (Psalm 119:105). As we uphold God's Word, our highest authority, and allow it to penetrate every corner of our mind and speak into every aspect of our lives, as we study the Scriptures from Genesis to Revelation—not as a series of isolated, disconnected stories and teachings but as a book with a single, comprehensive worldview—our minds are steadily transformed.

A transformed mind will naturally lead to a transformation in our behaviors and, ultimately, our entire lives. As John Stott says, "If we want to live straight, we have to think straight. If we want to think straight, we have to have renewed minds."[13] This is not an academic exercise. It is the essence of Christian discipleship. It is an essential part of the ongoing, lifelong process of sanctification. It is necessary if we are to be "salt and light" in the world (Matthew 5:13–16). For believers, there is nothing more important than the integrity of living according to God's revealed truth.

A COMPREHENSIVE WORLDVIEW

With that brief background on worldviews, let's return to our examination of ideological social justice. To rightly comprehend it, you have to see it for what it is: a comprehensive worldview. Christian apologist Neil Shenvi rightly says: "I worry that too many people are trying to hold on to both Christianity and critical theory. That's not going to work in the long run. We'll constantly be forced to choose between them in terms of values, priorities, and ethics. As we absorb the assumptions of critical theory, we will find that they inevitably erode core biblical truths."[14] I couldn't agree more.

In the next chapter, we'll dig into the core worldview presuppositions of ideological social justice, contrast them with those of the biblical worldview, and then evaluate them one at a time.

CHAPTER 5

THE IDEOLOGY'S CORE TENETS

ll worldviews have, at their core, a set of "givens" or presuppositions that frame everything else. These presuppositions typically answer the "big questions." What is ultimately real? Who are we? What is our fundamental problem as human beings? What is the solution to that problem? What's our purpose in life?

Ideological social justice provides answers to each of these questions and many more, giving shape to a comprehensive worldview.

I recognize that many sincere Christians are passionate about justice—I'm one of them—and have given their lives to fighting injustice and upholding the oppressed in the name of "social justice." If this is you, please know that I'm in no way implying that you hold to the presuppositions of ideological social justice I'm laying out here. My goal here is to help Christians understand that the phrase "social justice" is now the established label or brand in the broader culture for an entire worldview and to lay out its basic presuppositions.

	Ideological Social Justice	Biblical Worldview
What is ultimately real?	The *human mind* defines what is ultimately real.	The God of Genesis 1:1 defines ultimate reality: "In the beginning, God created the heavens and the earth."
Who are we?	Creatures whose identity is *wholly* socially determined. We are products of our race, sex, and gender identity.	Creations and image-bearers of a good, holy, and loving God with inherent dignity and immeasurable worth.
What is our fundamental problem as human beings?	Oppression: White, heteronormative males have established and maintain hegemonic power structures to oppress and subjugate women, people of color, and sexual minorities (LGBTQ+) and others.	Rebellion: *All have sinned*, and fallen short of the glory of God. Our rebellion against God has resulted in *broken relationships*—between God and man, between man and his fellow man, and between man and creation.
What is the solution to our problem?	Revolution: Oppressed victims and their allies must unite to unmask, deconstruct, and overthrow these oppressive power structures, systems, and institutions.	The gospel: On the cross, God incarnate bore the punishment we deserved for sinful rebellion in order to show us a mercy we could never deserve. His death on the cross and His resurrection opened the way for the reconciliation of all of our broken relationships.

	Ideological Social Justice	Biblical Worldview
How can we be saved?	Victims are morally innocent and do not require salvation. Oppressors can never be fully pardoned, but partial salvation is available if they confess their complicity in oppression and support the revolution.	"If you declare with your mouth, 'Jesus is Lord,' and believe in your heart that God raised him from the dead, you will be saved. … Everyone who calls on the name of the Lord will be saved." (Romans 10:9, 13)
What is our primary moral duty?	To stand in solidarity with, protect, and defend the oppressed: women, people of color, sexual minorities (LGBTQ+), etc.	To love God with all our heart, soul, mind, and strength (which involves living in obedience to all that Christ commanded) and to love our neighbors as ourselves.
How do we know what is true?	The notions of objective truth, reason, logic, evidence, and argument are discredited tools that oppressors employ to maintain their hegemony. We gain knowledge of "truth" through victims, who, based on their lived experience of oppression, have greater insight than oppressors. This is referred to as Standpoint Epistemology.	Divine revelation: (1) God's written Word (2 Timothy 3:13); (2) the "law written on our heart," or human conscience (Romans 2:15); and God's revelation in creation (Romans 1:20). To this we apply our God-given capacity for reason, logic, discussion, and debate to assemble and weigh evidence in pursuit of truth.

	Ideological Social Justice	Biblical Worldview
Who has ultimate authority?	*Victims are the final authority.* The claims of victims based on their subjective, lived experience must be believed without question.	God (and His revealed Word in Scripture) is the final authority.
Is there a future, final judgment?	No. There is no god who will return to punish the wicked and reward the upright. Rather, injustice must be rooted out here and now by those with the power to do so.	Yes. Jesus will return and accomplish perfect justice. He will preserve all that is good and rid the world of all that is evil. Until then, He extends mercy and forgiveness to sinful people.

Neil Shenvi is exactly right when he says that these are two distinct and incompatible worldviews. The fact that so many evangelicals have absorbed so many of the presuppositions of ideological social justice is a huge problem for the church. Shenvi notes that ideological social justice and Christianity conflict regarding basic questions of epistemology, identity, morality, and authority. The core principles of each are diametrically opposed.

Let's examine each of these competing worldview assumptions in more detail.

WHAT IS ULTIMATELY REAL?

Ideological social justice grounds reality, not in the biblical God of Genesis 1:1, or even in the reality of the material universe and natural laws. Rather, reality is grounded in the human mind. This postmodern view of reality essentially deifies subjective human perception.

This view of ultimate reality is powerfully captured by American social theorist Jeremy Rifkin:

> We no longer feel ourselves to be guests in someone else's home and therefore obliged to make our behavior conform with a set of preexisting cosmic rules. We make the rules. We establish the parameters of reality. We create the world, and because we do, we no longer feel beholden to outside forces. We no longer have to justify our behavior, for we are now the architects of the universe. We are responsible for nothing outside ourselves, for we are the kingdom, the power, and the glory forever.

Rifkin uses religious language to describe this postmodern view of reality. There is no God we are answerable to. There are no natural laws that we must conform to. We create reality. *We* are god. James Lindsay and Mike Nayna, in their article "Postmodern Religion and the Faith of Social Justice,"[1] describe ideological social justice as "applied postmodernism."

The biblical worldview, by contrast, grounds reality in the God who created the heavens and the earth. Nothing exists or makes sense apart from Him.

> For in him all things were created: things in heaven and on earth, visible and invisible, whether thrones or powers or rulers or authorities; all things have been created through him and for him. He is before all things, and in him all things hold together. (Colossians 1:16–17)

These two different starting points lead to two different and indeed irreconcilable worldviews. What Francis Schaeffer said about the conflict between a biblical worldview and a secular materialism in 1981 is equally true today in the conflict between the biblical worldview and ideological social justice:

> These two world views stand as totals in complete antithesis to each other in content and also in their natural results—including sociological and governmental results, and specifically including law. . . . It is not that these two world views are different only in how they understand the nature of reality and existence. They also inevitably produce totally different results. The operative word here is inevitably. It is not just that they happen to bring forth different results, but it is absolutely inevitable that they will bring forth different results.[2]

WHO ARE WE?

The biblical worldview asserts that human beings are creations of a holy, good, and loving God, and that we, both male and female, are made "in his image" and "likeness" (Genesis 1:26–28). As such, all people have a common human nature. They have intrinsic dignity and worth, as well as immutable rights to life and liberty.

Ideological social justice, by contrast, views human beings as creatures whose identity is *wholly* determined by group affiliations, particularly those based on race, sex, and so-called "gender identity" (LGBTQ+). There is no shared "human nature." Even more radical, there is no such thing as "the individual." Rather, our identity is entirely socially constructed.

In her book *Finding Truth*, Nancy Pearcey explains this social justice anthropology: "Everyone's ideas are . . . merely social constructions stitched together by cultural forces. Individuals are little more than mouthpieces for communities based on race, class, gender, ethnicity, and sexual identity."[3] Jordan Peterson agrees: ideological social justice "denies the existence of the individual . . . [it claims that] all you are is an avatar of your group interests." The ramifications of this idea are profound. Practically, it reduces "individuals to puppets of social forces . . . powerless to rise above the communities to which they belong."[4]

This helps explain why for LGBTQ+ individuals, their sexual activity isn't viewed as a choice, or a behavior, but an *identity*. It's not what I do, *it's who I am*. If you oppose someone's homosexuality in this view, you are denying his or her very humanity, akin to a Nazi dehumanizing a Jew or a slaveholder dehumanizing a slave. There is no forgiveness for such a person.

There is probably no more far-reaching belief in ideological social justice than its denial of the individual. Based on this radical presupposition, your personal history, life experiences, choices, and deeply held beliefs *don't matter*. The *only things* that matter in defining who you are, are your group affiliations. Individual freedom, responsibility, and accountability are all casualties of this profoundly destructive and dehumanizing belief.

By contrast, the Bible affirms the importance of every individual. All lives matter! God raises up individuals, such as Abraham, Moses, Ruth, Elijah, Jesus, Peter, Wilberforce, and you and me, to change the course of history. Our choices matter! God holds us individually accountable for our beliefs and actions (see Matthew 25:31–46 and Hebrews 4:13). At the final judgment, we won't be excused because we were members of a so-called victim group. Jesus warned some of his opponents that their identification as Jews would not save them, saying, "And do not presume to say to yourselves, 'We have Abraham as our father,' for I tell you, God is able from these stones to raise up children for Abraham" (Matthew 3:9).

As image-bearers of God, we have moral agency, and with our moral choices come responsibility and accountability. Ideological social justice denies all of this. This is not only dehumanizing—it is atomistic. People no longer have a shared humanity. No longer can we anticipate, as did Martin Luther King Jr., that "all God's children" will join hands and sing in unity.

This presupposition about human nature was put on display in a now infamous YouTube video that captured an angry confrontation between a group of Yale University students in 2015 and Professor Nicholas Christakis. At one point in the exchange, Christakis says to his interlocutors: "So I have a vision of us, as people, as human beings that actually privileges our common humanity . . . that is interested not in what is different among us, but what is the same." In response, a black student gets in his face and says: "Look me right in the eye. Look at me! Your experience will never connect to mine."[5]

The student is speaking from the assumption that race defines identity. Because Christakis is white, his experience "will never connect" to that of the black student's. If that is true, is discussion even possible?

Christians can agree with social justice advocates on one point: Human beings are shaped profoundly by groups. The Bible affirms that we are not merely individuals but are social beings made for relationships ("It is not good for the man to be alone" [Genesis 2:18]). We are part of groups (families, churches, ethnicities) that deeply shape who we are. We are acculturated into these groups by shared languages, values, habits, and histories.

But we forcefully deny that human identity can be reduced to group identity. The groups we belong to *shape* us. They do not *define* us. The bedrock of human identity is found in our common creation (we are all created in God's image and likeness, with equal value and dignity) and in God's gracious open door to redemption. We are all rebels, but God has opened a way for all people to be saved. When our relationship to God is restored through faith in Christ, we regain our true identity, one that transcends group identities:

> For in Christ Jesus you are all sons of God, through faith. For as many of you as were baptized into Christ have put on Christ. There is neither Jew nor Greek, there is neither slave nor free, there is no male and female, for you are all one in Christ Jesus. (Galatians 3:26–28 ESV)

In denying the existence of the individual, and claiming that our identity is wholly defined by the groups we belong to, ideological social justice repudiates the essential idea that grounds Western civilization. If this dehumanizing and dangerous idea carries the day, the cultural consequences will be far more devastating than we can imagine. The Judeo-Christian worldview that shaped Western civilization is, at root, based on the idea that we have a shared, common human nature, and at the same time, human individuality profoundly matters, because every single person is a special and unique creation of God, bearing His holy image.

This biblical idea created the West, and none of us can fully imagine the dystopia that would result if we discard it in favor of the dehumanizing idea that individuals don't exist, and that people are reduced to mouthpieces, drones, or avatars of the groups that define them. In this fraught cultural moment, we need to emphasize what unites us, not what divides us. Let's follow the examples of Martin Luther King Jr. and Nelson Mandela, who led healing movements that brought wounded nations together. They sought to unite people around our common humanity.

Ideological social justice can only divide because it has no basis for unity. It can only segregate us into competing tribes, pitted against each other in an endless power struggle.

WHAT IS OUR FUNDAMENTAL PROBLEM AS HUMAN BEINGS?

For believers in social justice, the answer can be expressed in one word: "Oppression."

In this worldview, evil doesn't originate in the human heart. There is no doctrine of the fall or human depravity. Rather, evil is sourced outside of man, in society, and specifically in social structures, systems, institutions, laws, and cultural norms that perpetuate inequalities and grant one group power and privileges at the expense of others.

We've just looked at how ideological social justice defines people entirely according to the groups they belong to. It then goes on to assert that all these diverse groups are pitted against one another in a kind of Hobbesian, zero-sum competition for power. In this struggle, one group presently has supremacy: white, heteronormative males. They've accomplished this feat over centuries by establishing a complex web of societal structures, systems, institutions, laws, and norms that "advantage" them at the expense of everyone else, particularly, "people of color," women, and "sexual minorities" (LGBTQ+). These interlocking webs of systemic oppression have many labels: white supremacy," "toxic masculinity," and "the patriarchy" are just a few.

For influential *Atlantic* essayist Ta-Nehisi Coates, our fundamental human problem is "whiteness" which he describes as "an existential danger to the country and the world." Quoting his hero, cultural critic James Baldwin, he claims ominously that "whites have brought humanity to the edge of oblivion." According to Coates, "The power of domination and exclusion is central to the belief in being white, and without it, 'white people' would cease to exist for want of reasons."[6]

Coates's views cannot be dismissed as "fringe" or outside the mainstream. He writes for a venerable and respected publication. He is regularly praised by respected public figures, such as President Barack Obama. Carlos Lozada of the *Washington Post* even called him "America's foremost public intellectual."[7] Evangelical pastors, such as Ken Wytsma, founder of the Justice Conference, describe Coates's writings as "must-read."

Silicon Valley tech titan and LGBTQ+ activist Tim Gill sources the evil in this world back to the Judeo-Christian sexual ethic. He uses his enormous wealth to push for LGBTQ+ rights across the nation, describing his crusade this way: "We're going into the hardest states in the country. We're going [to work to pass sexual orientation and gender identity bills] *to punish the wicked*" (italics added).[8]

Who are "the wicked" oppressors? Those—mostly religious conservatives—who uphold male-female marriage and the natural family.

Then there are those like essayist and feminist activist Philippe Leonard Fradet, who source evil in masculinity and "the patriarchy." He writes:

> What all of this comes down to is the simple fact that the masculinity that patriarchy has bred and enabled is extremely toxic. It makes everything worse . . . for those who are subjected to all of its negativity, hatred, subordination, and oppression.[9]

This dividing of the world into oppressors and victims has given rise to the concept of *intersectionality*. Alan Jacobs describes it this way. Intersectionality occurs when "someone who belongs to more than one oppressed or marginalized group—a black lesbian, for instance—experiences such oppression or marginalization in a particularly intensified way thanks to the 'intersection' of those social forces."[10] In short, the more victim boxes you can check, the greater your experience of oppression.

Ideologies that draw the good vs. evil line between different groups are not just wrong, they are dangerous. If this group is good, and that group is evil, it is very easy to dehumanize the "evil" group. This is what happened in Nazi Germany with the Jews and in communist nations with "capitalists." It happened in Rwanda in 1994, when the Hutu-led government, fueled by an ideology of hate, launched a genocide that left as many as a million Tutsis dead in just one hundred days.

Followers of Jesus Christ must never be complicit in an ideology that encourages the dehumanization of our neighbors, particularly when the dehumanization is based on an immutable characteristic such as skin color.

As former intelligence analyst Stella Morabito observes:

Railing against an entire [group] of people . . . ultimately means rejecting each and every individual in that supposed category, regardless of the personal experiences or human sufferings any one of them might have endured as an individual. . . .

That's a hideous effect, because it is that very balance that makes human relationships possible. . . .

Why should one person's immutable characteristic cancel out their entire experience as an individual human being? How is that not the essence of bigotry? How is that not pre-judging and de-humanizing a person?[11]

In one of his most controversial statements, Ta-Nehisi Coates describes to his son his reaction to watching the New York City police and fire fighters rush into the World Trade Center buildings on 9/11. "*They were not human to me.* Black, white, or whatever, they were menaces of nature; they were the fire, the comet, the storm, which could—with no justification—shatter my body"[12] (italics added). Here you see not only Coates's inability to see people as individuals—as fellow human beings. His worldview reduces them to subhuman representatives of oppressive groups.

Despite the best intentions of its adherents—and many *do* have good intentions—ideological social justice destroys civil, humane society, replacing it with hatred, division, and tribalism. Unless we wake up to its dangers, social justice will destroy us— and it will do so in the name of "justice."

How different all of this is from the biblical worldview. What is our fundamental problem as human beings? It is not systemic oppression by white, straight males. Our one-word answer isn't "oppression" but "rebellion." "All have sinned and fall short of the glory of God" (Romans 3:23). Our fundamental problem is that we—*all of us*—are in a state of open rebellion against our Creator. Romans chapter one lays out our fundamental human problem in no uncertain terms:

> For although [mankind] knew God, they did not honor him as God or give thanks to him, but they became futile in their thinking, and their foolish hearts were darkened. Claiming to be wise, they became fools, and exchanged the glory of the immortal God for images resembling mortal man and birds and animals and creeping things. . .
>
> And since they did not see fit to acknowledge God, God gave them up to a debased mind to do what ought not to be done. They were filled with all manner of unrighteousness, evil, covetousness, malice. They are full of envy, murder, strife, deceit, maliciousness. They are gossips, slanderers, haters of God, insolent, haughty, boastful, inventors of evil, disobedient to parents, foolish, faithless, heartless, ruthless. (Romans 1:21–23, 28–31 ESV)

Paul couldn't be clearer. Our fundamental problem is not "out there" in oppressive societal structures. Our problem is "in here," in our foolish, darkened hearts. All of us are implicated. Evil is sourced in our rebellious human hearts from which flow all manner of unrighteousness and evil. In the immortal words of Aleksandr Solzhenitsyn: "The line separating good and evil passes not through states, nor between classes, nor between political parties either—*but right through every human heart*" (emphasis added).[13]

We all have sinned and rebelled against our Creator. Every problem we face: broken relationships, broken marriages and families, hatred, envy, violence, war, and, yes, systemic oppression, all stem from a deeper spring: our rebellion and alienation from God.

WHAT IS THE SOLUTION TO OUR PROBLEM?

"Revolution" is the answer that ideological social justice gives. Oppressed victims and their allies must unite in an intersectional coalition to unmask, deconstruct, and ultimately overthrow oppressive power structures.

At the 2018 Human Rights Campaign awards banquet, Hollywood actress Anne Hathaway expressed this boldly in her speech accepting the National Equality Award. With tears in her eyes, she spoke about the "myth of centering reality around whiteness." She said:

> It is important to acknowledge with the exception of being a cisgender male, everything about how I was born has put me at the current center of a damaging and widely accepted myth.
>
> That myth is that gayness orbits around straightness, transgender orbits around cisgender, and that all races orbit around whiteness.
>
> . . . Together we are not going to just question this myth, *we are going to destroy it.*
>
> . . . *Let's tear this world apart and build a better one.* (italics added)[14]

More often than not, social justice champions are seeking not a peaceful social transformation that begins inwardly with humble repentance and the regeneration of sinful hearts and minds. Like Hathaway, they want nothing less than a revolution. And the revolution they champion is based on the patterns established by the French, Russian, and Chinese revolutions. The old, often Jewish and Christian, ideas and traditions of Western civilization need to be "destroyed" to make way for the new.

Karl Marx, of course, was a committed revolutionary. His great aim was to tear down the oppressive capitalist system and build his communist utopia. Social justice ideology takes it a step farther—make that several steps! It seeks the overthrow of systemic white-supremacy, the patriarchy, and Judeo-Christian morality. This revolutionary zeal drives one side of our ongoing culture war. While many social justice advocates, such as Hathaway, say they want to build a better world, they seem far more animated about tearing the existing one down.

According to Rod Dreher, the social justice revolution is "great at tearing down what we have . . . [but doesn't] offer much to replace it." He then quotes political theorist Augusto Del Noce: "the new [neo-Marxist] totalitarianism . . . dominates by disintegrating."[15] Social justice revolutionaries talk constantly about "subverting" or "dismantling" or "deconstructing" any manner of cultural, economic, or institutional systems or institutions that are claimed to propagate oppression.

The tactics of social justice revolutionaries are typically exercises in raw power reminiscent of Mao's Cultural Revolution or George Orwell's dystopian novel 1984. While of course there are exceptions (particularly among evangelical joiners), mainstream social justice tactics include compulsory reeducation and indoctrination (often called "sensitivity training"), innuendo, contempt, threats, shaming, silencing, and mob actions.

Having rejected the Judeo-Christian foundations of society, social justice advocates have no basis for treating ideological opponents with respect as image-bearers of God. Peggy Noonan observes that in America today,

> the air is full of accusation and humiliation. We have seen this spirit most famously on the campuses, where students protest harshly, sometimes violently, views they wish to suppress. Social media is full of swarming political and ideological mobs. In an interesting departure from democratic tradition, [social justice revolutionaries] don't try to win the other side over. They only condemn and attempt to silence.[16]

Political correctness is perhaps the most familiar tactic of social justice revolutionaries. PC is shorthand for speech codes (written or unwritten) wielded to silence opposing viewpoints and cow or humiliate those who hold them. Political correctness, supposedly a way to shield the oppressed, is used to inflict penalties on violators—public defamation, shaming, fines, the loss of employment or reputation, and mandatory reeducation (under the guise of sensitivity training). All this is simply a precursor to policies and laws that ban unacceptable viewpoints and anyone with the temerity to espouse them.

In the zero-sum world of social justice power struggle, there is no "live and let live" tolerance. No win-win, or even compromise. No place for forgiveness, or grace. No "love your enemy." No "first get the log out of your own eye" introspection. There is only grievance, condemnation, and retribution. Bigots, haters, and oppressors must be destroyed.

Those who uphold the biblical worldview agree with social justice revolutionaries on this: Our societies are broken and need to change! With all the injustice in the world, all the suffering, pain, and heartbreak, we need cultural transformation. The status quo is not acceptable. Yes, there are oppressive systems, structures, and institutions. We cannot stand idly by while these things continue destroying people and despoiling God's magnificent creation. As one of the prophets declared in a time much like our own, "But let justice roll down like waters, / and righteousness like an ever-flowing stream" (Amos 5:24 ESV).

Where we have irreconcilable differences, however, is on how this change should come about.

What solution does the Bible offer to our fundamental human problem? That problem is broken relationships and, fundamentally, alienation from our Creator—the wellspring of all the brokenness that exists in the world. Until this root problem is addressed, there is no possibility for lasting social change.

The breathtakingly good news is that hope for forgiveness and reconciliation with God is available! God Himself has taken the initiative in reconciling with His rebellious children. The glorious solution to our fundamental human problem is the gospel:

> For God so loved the world, that he gave his only Son, that whoever believes in him should not perish but have eternal life. For God did not send his Son into the world to condemn the world, but in order that the world might be saved through him. (John 3:16–17 ESV)

On the cross, God incarnate bore the punishment we deserved for our sinful rebellion in order to show us a mercy we could never deserve. The cross and resurrection opened the way for the reconciliation of our broken relationship with God, and all of our other broken relationships as well.

A big reason for our differing approaches, as we have seen, is that social justice ideology sources evil in social structures. We find it, by contrast, in human hearts and demonic forces. They see evil as social. We see it as personal. Unjust people create, sustain, and perpetuate unjust systems and structures for selfish ends.

Ultimately, injustice isn't a social problem. It is a moral problem. Injustice exists because we are all fallen, sinful, selfish people. The only solution is a personal, heart-level transformation, not just for a particular group of so-called "oppressors," but for everyone. Biblical transformation encompasses both the inward and the outward, the personal and the societal, the regeneration of fallen human hearts and minds and the reformation of society.

Biblical social change is an *inside-out* process that begins with inward transformation. First John 1:9 (NASB) says that "If we confess our sins, He is faithful and righteous to forgive us our sins and to cleanse us from all unrighteousness." As we respond to the Holy Spirit's leading and accept the free gift of forgiveness in Christ, God works the miracle foretold by the prophet Ezekiel: "I will give you a new heart and put a new spirit in you; I will remove from you your heart of stone and give you a heart of flesh" (Ezekiel 36:26). This is where the process of genuine social transformation begins.

This divine act of heart-level regeneration is followed by God's work of sanctification, leading to a transformed character. All of this inward, personal transformation then ripples outward into the social spheres: marriage, family relationships, close friends, vocational areas, institutional reform, and ultimately nations.

Genuine societal change can never neglect heart and mind transformation. Certainly, institutional evils such as slavery, abortion, corruption, pornography, and sex trafficking are real and must be opposed. But we have no hope for lasting social change apart from the gospel and new life in Christ. As Dallas Willard wisely said, the revolution of Jesus is

> a revolution of the human heart or spirit. It did not and does not proceed by means of the formation of social institutions and laws. . . . Rather, it is a revolution of character, which proceeds by changing people from the inside through ongoing personal relationship to God in Christ and to one another. It is one that changes their ideas, beliefs, feelings, and habits of choice, as well as their . . . social relations. . . . From these divinely renovated depths of the person, social structures will naturally be transformed so that "justice roll[s] down like waters and righteousness like an ever-flowing stream" (Amos 5:24).[17]

Yes, we long to see our broken, impoverished, hurting societies healed. But the solutions provided by social justice advocates only make things worse by misdiagnosing the problem. It isn't the patriarchy or "whiteness," and it certainly isn't biblical sexual morality. Unjust and oppressive human systems, structures, institutions, laws, and norms are symptoms, not the disease. The disease is sin. It is alienation from God and the resulting alienations that flow from that—alienation from ourselves, our neighbors, and creation itself. The solution is inward heart and mind transformation through the gospel, leading to outward, societal transformation.

"Our primary means of transforming the world is through proclaiming the gospel," says pastor Grover Gunn. "We must today never question the effectiveness of the gospel message as the cutting edge of positive social change."[18] John Stott agrees: "Evangelism is the major instrument of social change. For the gospel changes people, and changed people can change society."[19]

Christianity's ethic of humility, personal responsibility, love, and forgiveness fosters reconciliation. Social justice's ethic is based on grievance and a desire to blame others for the world's problems. It brings to mind this insight from C. S. Lewis: "We must picture hell as a state where everyone . . . has a grievance, and where everyone lives in the deadly serious passions of envy . . . and resentment."[20] This pretty well describes ideological social justice. It has no basis for love, forgiveness, or reconciliation. It destroys relationships and tears apart the social fabric. Christians, whose job is to love our neighbors and bless the nations, must recognize and reject this destructive worldview as we attempt, in God's strength, to live out a "more excellent way."

WHAT IS OUR PRIMARY MORAL DUTY?

Social justice, like Marxism, rejects the idea of an objective, transcendent, universal morality. It asserts that human beings are autonomous—laws unto themselves. Morality in this system doesn't vanish. As image-bearers of God, a moral sense is deeply embedded in our human nature. We need a system of morality much like we need air and water.

But a morality that is untethered from God is continually in flux and utterly arbitrary. At the societal level, moral norms change as particular groups amass cultural power and influence, establish dominant narratives that drive popular opinion, and implement changes in policies and legal codes.

As ideological social justice has become the dominant worldview in the West, this is exactly what has happened. Morality hasn't gone away. Far from it! Instead, over the past decade, we've experienced nothing short of a moral revolution. Things that were formerly understood to be good—such as, freedom of speech; freedom of religion; reserving sex until marriage; marriage as the exclusive, lifelong union of a man and a woman; and even the male-female binary itself—are increasingly understood to be bad. They are bigoted, hateful, discriminatory—tools of oppression.

Take the "gay rights" movement. Until the mid-twentieth century in America, homosexuality was widely understood to be immoral. After the AIDS crisis of the 1980s, homosexual activists became more visible and vocal, telling their stories and appropriating the language of love, commitment, marriage, and civil rights.[21] A series of prohomosexual characters and story lines in pop culture and the media lowered defenses and combatted stereotypes too.

The Pew Research Center notes that a minority of 46 percent of Americans thought homosexuality should be accepted by society in 1994. By 2017, the share supporting homosexuality had ballooned to a supermajority of 70 percent.[22] No wonder that Barack Obama, who for most of his political career publicly opposed marriage between homosexuals, in 2012 famously "evolved," becoming the first president to support it.[23] The *Obergefell* decision of the Supreme Court in 2015 recognizing homosexual marriage cemented these trends into law.

In the blink of an eye, what was understood to be immoral is now moral, a positive good to be publicly celebrated. The reverse is also true. If you uphold the former moral order by refusing to celebrate LGBTQ+ behavior based on your religious convictions, this makes you an *immoral* person—hateful, bigoted, homo/transphobic, and increasingly subject to civil penalties. This is what a growing cadre of Christian bakers, florists, fast-food purveyors, and adoption agencies has learned. Today, what is intolerable is the belief in an objective moral standard rooted in God's law.

Jayme Metzgar perceptively describes the new social justice morality:

> Without God's goodness as a plumb line for right and wrong, moderns have no framework with which to judge the clear evils that exist in human behavior. So they've settled on a simplistic moral standard that boils all sin down to a single category: oppression.[24]

This is exactly right. According to ideological social justice, the primary moral duty of humankind is to fight oppression—specifically, the systemic oppression propagated by white, straight males against their so-called victims.

On matters of race, for example, we have a new moral obligation to fight against "whiteness" or "white privilege," which are viewed as a kind of original sin. White people need to be educated and made conscious of (or "woke to") their white privilege, inherent and unconscious racism, and white supremacy. To challenge any of these assumptions (to "whitesplain") is merely to demonstrate your "white fragility." Defending oneself against charges of racism and other social justice sins, when leveled by someone from an oppressed group, is verboten. As Rod Dreher says drily, "Resistance to the claim that you are guilty is evidence of your guilt."[25]

Privilege, in this moral framework, isn't something you experience as an individual. It is wholly associated with group identity. If you are a white male, you are, by definition, privileged. This is true regardless of your history or circumstances. If you were raised in a broken home, in a neighborhood rife with drug addiction, poverty, and violence, you are still privileged. Likewise, if you are a "person of color" or a female, or a "sexual minority" and were raised in an intact family, born into wealth, with all the benefits the best education can afford, you are still a victim.

Bear in mind that privilege is indeed real. Some people do have more privilege than others, however the line of privilege should never be drawn exclusively on the basis of skin color.

Ironically, white people are often the biggest promoters of this new racial morality. Some explain this as "white guilt" over very real past injustices perpetrated against black people, including slavery and Jim Crow. No doubt there is some truth in this, but a better explanation is that many white people are simply jumping on board the new moral bandwagon, publicly announcing to everyone that they are on "the right side of history." They've learned that if you confess your inherent racism and privilege, you signal to cultural gatekeepers that you are morally superior to the unwoke masses. This explains the phenomenon of Pharisee-like "virtue-signaling" or publicly and proudly proclaiming your fealty to the new social justice moral code.

The pressure to conform is immense, particularly in places where the social justice worldview is the unquestioned paradigm (university campuses, corporate boardrooms, and urban centers on both coasts). Those who fail to jump on the new moral bandwagon are branded *immoral*—unenlightened, hateful, and bigoted.

There is no place in this moral order for grace or forgiveness. The new morality is ruthlessly enforced, not so much by government officials (at least not yet), as by private groups, corporations, associations, professional credentialing agencies, internet and social media titans, and others. "Woke" social media mobs roam the internet on the lookout for the slightest moral slipup. Say the wrong thing, or donate to the wrong cause, or associate with the wrong people, and you might be banned on social media, lose your job, or even your reputation.

In contrast to the biblical framework in which our debt to God is fully repaid by Christ's death on the cross (Colossians 2:14–15), social justice oppressors carry debts that can *never* be fully expunged. When asked whether reparations (to the tune of billions of dollars transferred from whites to blacks) would balance the scales of justice for the injustice of slavery, Ta-Nehisi Coates replied that "the country *can never* fully repay African-Americans."[26] For Coates, there is no forgiveness for white people, only eternal penance.

In the new morality of ideological social justice, guilt belongs not to humankind as a whole, but to one group only: white, heteronormative males. Because people are not responsible moral agents, but victims or beneficiaries of oppressive systems, guilt or innocence are not a function of individual choices, but group identity. If you are a victim, you are morally innocent. If you are an oppressor, you are morally guilty, regardless of your actions.

According to the theory of intersectionality:

Victimhood is the highest virtue. Victims and members of oppressed identity groups are elevated to a kind of sainthood. . . . This is in fact exactly what intersectionality teaches, complete with a hierarchy of victimhood for comparing everyone's relative righteousness.[27]

We've seen how this destructive idea has played out in history. During the Russian Revolution, if you were a member of the property-owning class, you were, by definition, guilty, convicted, and sent to the gulag—regardless of your personal actions. Even if you never cheated anyone and were generous to the poor—none of that mattered. The only thing that mattered in determining guilt or innocence was group affiliation—in this case, class. If you were a member of the working class, you were morally innocent, and rewarded with the confiscated property of the morally guilty bourgeoisie. This gross injustice was undertaken in the name of justice.

The false system of moral guilt and innocence at the heart of social justice morality makes it incompatible with the gospel. In fact, it is a false gospel. The Bible teaches that every human being, regardless of sex, gender, or skin color, is a sinner who needs God's forgiveness (Romans 3:23; 6:23). While the consequences of sin may be passed down from one generation to another (Jeremiah 32:18), the guilt of sin is earned individually (Ezekiel 18:20). Though God loves people of every ethnic group (Revelation 7:9), He is no respecter of persons (Acts 10:34), and no one will get a pass from Him based upon membership in any particular group (Galatians 3:28). Salvation is by grace through faith (Ephesians 2:8–9).

As followers of Jesus Christ, we should react the same way to social justice morality that the apostle Paul reacted to the false gospels in his day: "But even if we or an angel from heaven should preach to you a gospel contrary to the one we preached to you, let him be accursed" (Galatians 1:8 ESV).

What is our primary moral duty, according to the biblical worldview? To love God with all our heart, soul, mind, and strength, and to love our neighbors as ourselves (Matthew 22:37–40). Loving God means obeying His commands (John 14:15), and loving our neighbors certainly involves caring for the plight of oppressed people. This was Jesus's point in the parable of the good Samaritan. We are morally obligated to care for truly oppressed and victimized people. However, the Bible doesn't define victims or oppressors in the same way that ideological social justice does. Oppressors are certainly not exclusively white men, nor are victims exclusively people of color, women, or LGBTQ members. In the Bible, victims look a lot more like the man beaten up, robbed, and left to die alongside the road in the parable of the good Samaritan.

Yes, we have a moral duty to care for oppressed and victimized people, but we have to understand who these people are biblically—not according to the presuppositions of ideological social justice. We also have to be careful not to categorically view representatives of powerful, often oppressive systems as irredeemably evil. God shows His love to such people throughout the Scripture. Jesus sought out and forgave Zacchaeus, a hated tax collector and traitorous agent of the powerful, cruel, and oppressive Roman Empire. He befriended Nicodemus, a powerful member of the Sanhedrin that eventually condemned Him to death. He even chose Cornelius, a powerful Roman solider, to be among the first Christians, commanding Peter to welcome him into the fledgling, largely Jewish church. If God can extend His grace to people who are part of oppressor groups, so should we.

Finally, as Christ-followers, we must uphold the biblical idea of morality as objective and rooted in God's character and His Word, which is the final authority. Any form of justice not grounded in God's law will result in injustice, for it is based on fallen human reason.

HOW DO WE KNOW WHAT IS TRUE?

At root, ideological social justice is atheistic. Because God does not exist, according to this ideology, objective truth doesn't exist. Everything is relative to the "identity group." There are no fixed points—no publicly authoritative facts or truths that transcend groups or cultures. There are only perspectives or interpretations—your group's truth, or my group's truth, but no longer *the* truth. As Nancy Pearcey explains, "Truth has been redefined as a social construction, so that every community has its own view of truth, based on its experience and perspective, which cannot be judged by anyone outside the community."[28]

This is not to say that each group's views are *equally* true however. Academic critical theory has given rise to the concept of Standpoint Epistemology. Simply put, the greater a group's experience of intersectional oppression, the greater its members' insight into reality. Standpoint Epistemology "makes three central claims: (1) knowledge is socially situated, (2) marginalized groups have an advantage in being able to spot biases that the dominant group cannot see, and (3) knowledge should be built upon the marginalized perspectives.[29]

For social justice ideologues, the very notions of objective truth, reason, logic, evidence, and argument are viewed as weapons employed by oppressors to maintain their hegemony. When reason and logic are discarded, "feelings" and emotions take center stage. Discussion and debate to discover the truth are replaced with hyperbolic claims of emotional duress. "Hurt feelings" are all that are required to defeat opponents. Robert Tracinski says this appeal to emotion is "specifically designed to make rational analysis of the issues look . . . positively immoral."[30] In the confrontation at Yale University referred to earlier, Nicholas Christakis asked the students, "Who gets to decide what [language] is offensive? Who decides?" A female student answered: "When it hurts me." Case closed.

Leading-edge thinkers, such as John Corvino, a professor of philosophy at Wayne State University, are laying the groundwork for *dignitary harm* to replace *material harm* (physical injury, stolen or damaged property, etc.) as a legal standard for prosecution and punishment by the state. Corvino defines *dignity harm* as:

> (1) treating people as inferior, regardless of whether anyone recognizes the mistreatment; (2) causing people to feel inferior, intentionally or not; and (3) contributing to systemic moral inequality, intentionally or not.[31]

That's right—hurting someone's feelings would be actionable. Today, if you dare to argue that differences between men and women are essential and complementary in marriage and family, or that marriage is linked intrinsically to procreation (which requires male and female), or that children need the loving care of both mothers and fathers, who bring essential, yet different strengths to parenting, you might expect to be accused of causing someone dignitary harm. If it becomes a legal standard, such arguments would become illegal. If you argue that the male-female binary objectively exists and isn't a matter of choice—that you are not "assigned" a sex at birth, but are born either male or female with distinct biological, physiological, and psychological differences that must be acknowledged and respected, you might go to jail.

As Nancy Pearcey explains, "If there is no objective or universal truth, then any claim to have objective truth will be treated as nothing but an attempt by one . . . community to impose its own limited, subjective perspective on everyone else. An act of oppression. A power grab."[32] James Lindsay agrees. According to the social justice ideologue, "What we believe to be 'true' is in large part a function of social power: who wields it, who's oppressed by it, how it influences which messages we hear."[33] In true Orwellian fashion, ideological social justice reduces truth to power. Whoever has the power to impose a dominant narrative has the power to define "truth." When objective truth is abandoned, narratives thrive.

Narratives are man-made "stories" that purport to describe reality but are agenda-driven. They appeal to emotions over reason by painting with broad brushstrokes. They reduce nuanced, complex, multifaceted realities into simple, black-and-white, good versus evil plotlines. They come complete with clear-cut villains and victims. The victims, naturally, are women, people of color, or members of the LGBTQ+ community. Villains are nearly always straight, white males. The gut-level appeal of narratives gives them a certain power. People want to believe them. They work by employing distortion. While they may have some basis in fact, the supporting evidence is cherry-picked, while other facts that call the plotline into question are suppressed and ignored.

A particularly egregious example used to further a social justice agenda was the Michael Brown, "Hands up, don't shoot!"

narrative in Ferguson, Missouri. It was a catalyst that gave rise to the Black Lives Matter movement. Because Brown was black, he was cast as a victim of wanton police brutality. Because the officer, Darren Wilson, was white, he was cast as a villain even before the facts of the case were known. According to this carefully crafted narrative, Brown innocently approached Wilson's patrol car with his hands raised, pleading, "Hands up, don't shoot!" Wilson proceeded to gun him down anyway. None of this was true, as a grand jury discovered in acquitting Wilson and according to a later in-depth investigation by the Barack Obama / Eric Holder Department of Justice. But by that time, it was too late. The popular narrative was already well established and continues to be accepted as "truth" by many to this day. Objective truth, eyewitness testimony, investigation, evidence, and legal verdicts are of little importance when one operates in the worldview of ideological social justice. Those who try to uncover the truth are, in fact, often demonized.

It's hard to overstate just how destructive all of this is. Truth, and a basic sense of honesty, is a glue that holds societies together. Weaken that bond, and things quickly fall apart. By denying objective truth, and devaluing logic, reason, facts, and evidence, ideological social justice actively and intentionally weakens the bonds of our society.

Without truth, as the late Ravi Zacharias rightly tells us, there is no justice. With truth untethered from God and inextricably linked to the narratives of the culturally powerful, there is no true justice for those who refuse to toe the party line. What is called social justice is too often actually a perversion of justice. In fact, the increasing influence of social justice ideology is weakening one of the main supports of Western civilization—due process, the very bedrock of our system of justice in a civil society.

There is no presumption of innocence if you belong to the wrong group or espouse the wrong opinions. Frankly, with the new social justice intersectional hierarchy, if you are a white male, you are presumed guilty. Forget a careful search for evidence and supporting facts "beyond a reasonable doubt" before a verdict is rendered. Even demonstrably false charges get the benefit of the doubt if they are made by a member of a victim group. Gone also is the right to face your accuser, to cross-examine witnesses, to produce evidence on your behalf, and most significantly, to be presumed innocent until proven guilty.

The Western concept of due process, rooted in the Judeo-Christian worldview, is a cultural achievement that was centuries in the making. Unless it is defended against the onslaught of ideological social justice, it can vanish in one generation. We take it for granted at our peril.

Truth, by contrast, is a central, load-bearing pillar of the Christian worldview. The great Founder of our faith made that abundantly clear: "I am the way and the truth and the life" (John 14:6), Jesus said. He later said that "the reason I was born and came into the world is to testify to the truth. Everyone on the side of truth listens to me" (John 18:37). God exists as the Creator of the cosmos—the ultimate fixed point. And because He exists, truth exists—absolute, objective, transcendent truth. God created each of us in His image to thrive in the truth, and to be truth-knowing, truth-telling creatures.

Without this Judeo-Christian commitment to objective, knowable truth, there would be no university. Nor would there be modern science, nor journalism, nor the study of history. There would be no liberal democracy, for without truth, government becomes an exercise in raw power. Professor Sinan Aral at the

Massachusetts Institute of Technology is *exactly* right: "Some notion of truth is central to the proper functioning of nearly every realm of human endeavor. If we allow the world to be consumed by falsity, we are inviting catastrophe."[34]

Truth is known through a combination of Divine revelation supported by the proper use of our God-given capacity for reason and logic, evidence and argument. As the church fathers put it, God's revelation comes to us in "two books"—the book of God's Word (the Bible), and the book of God's world (creation). We can add to this a third "book," the book of human reason and the internal witness of conscience, or "the law written on [our] hearts" (Romans 2:15). We search out the truth through the careful study of God's creation using the tools and methods of science, as well as the careful study of God's written Word through the principles of sound hermeneutics and with the indispensable illumination of the Holy Spirit.

Because we are finite, our capacity to know truth is limited. We are fallen, rebellious creatures, and thus prone to lies and deception. Yet despite these limitations, truth exists, and through diligent effort we can know it, imperfectly, incompletely, but truly.

The entire edifice of Western jurisprudence is based on this conviction. When witnesses testify in a court of law, they swear to "tell the truth, the whole truth, and nothing but the truth." When someone is accused of wrongdoing, we are taught not to prejudge until the facts and evidence are presented and carefully evaluated. Western civilization depicts "Lady Justice" wearing a blindfold, which points to the hard-won truth that justice must be impartial and not a respecter of persons. Everyone is equal before the law. Social justice ideology, however, is anything but blind, and proudly so. People are treated differently based on the groups to which they are assigned. Verdicts of guilt or innocence are largely based not on individual behavior, but on group affiliation. Narrative takes precedence over fact.

The Bible speaks out strongly against such partiality. "You shall do no injustice in court. You shall not be partial to the poor or defer to the great, but in righteousness shall you judge your neighbor" (Leviticus 19:15 ESV). See also Deuteronomy 10:17; Romans 2:11; Proverbs 24:23; and James 2:1–9.

True justice treats all people the same, regardless of skin color, ethnicity, sex, gender, or any other immutable characteristic. The Bible teaches that in a legal setting, guilt can only be determined on the basis of witnesses (Deuteronomy 19:15), and those witnesses must speak truthfully. Bearing false witness is a grave violation of the Ten Commandments (Exodus 20:16). Biblical justice is committed to discovering truth about guilt or innocence based on actions and behavior, not on membership in a so-called oppressor group.

And we must not forget that the perpetuation of distorted narratives by treating them as "truth," is just another form of lying. Narrative creators cherry-pick only those facts that fit their predetermined story lines and ignore or whitewash out those that don't. This is willful deception and must be roundly rejected by Christians. We have a bedrock commitment to truth telling, and truth seeking, in the conviction that truth exists, and all truth is God's truth. So we must never succumb to the postmodern practice of trafficking in false or distorted narratives in order to achieve a desired outcome.

"We don't create the truth; we find it, and we have no power to change it to our tastes," said Charles Chaput,[35] the

Roman Catholic Archbishop of Philadelphia. Rather, with impartiality, we must question popular cultural narratives out of a commitment to follow facts and evidence wherever they lead.

WHO HAS ULTIMATE AUTHORITY?

In the worldview of ideological social justice, authority is conferred, not by wisdom, age, position, or experience—but by victim status. Claims of oppression and victimization based on a subjective "lived experience" must be believed without question. The more intersectional victim-boxes one can check, the greater the moral authority. The greater the authority, the greater the power.

The empowering of victims naturally (and perversely) results in an explosion in the demand for victim status. Some have called it a veritable victimhood Olympics. Would-be victims are constantly on the lookout for opportunities to be claim offense or harm, searching out ever smaller "microagressions" to claim victimization. Even events that happened hundreds of years in the past are held against the offspring of those who perpetuated them. An increasing number of people, such as Jussie Smollett, are resorting to hate crime hoaxes to claim their victim bona fides along with the ensuring benefits.

Jonathan Haidt, professor of ethical leadership at New York University, has seen this tactic employed with greater frequency by his students, who "respond to even the slightest unintentional offense, even going so far as to falsify offenses."[36] According to *The Atlantic*, this is all part of "a new moral code in American life"—victimhood culture.[37]

This tactic works, in part, because most people rightly sympathize with victims, particularly in a society shaped by a biblical worldview that sees compassion for hurting people as virtuous. Social justice ideology, however, like a parasite, feeds off of our good and necessary compassion for true victims while twisting it to the advantage of favored groups.

Authority is closely connected to power, so it is important to grasp how ideological social justice understands both. As we've already established, in a world without God, objective truth, or transcendent morality, all that remains is power, which explains why ideological social justice is obsessed with power. Everything can be explained by power dynamics. The quest for power lurks behind all human interaction. Everything is reduced to the political.

A foundational belief in both the older Marxism and the newer ideology of social justice is the conviction that power and authority exist for one purpose, and one purpose only: to establish hegemony—to gain advantage over those with less power. In the worldview of ideological social justice, power is zero-sum. The powerful are the privileged at the expense of the unprivileged and powerless. If one group gains, another must lose. In this framework, history is nothing more than an endless saga of power and domination, with each group working by any means necessary to wrest power away groups that possess it.

In our present moment, ideological social justice sees power as held *exclusively* by white, straight men who maintain their hegemony through a vast, often hidden array of social systems: white supremacy, the patriarchy, and traditionally Western notions of marriage, family, and sexuality. The goal of the social justice revolution is to dismantle oppressive structures and transfer power and authority to victims. Victims only win when oppressors lose. That's how it works.

These core social justice assumptions about authority and power are grounded in an even deeper source of authority: the postmodern academic discipline of *critical theory* or *grievance studies*, which gained prominence after World War II through the efforts of the neo-Marxist Frankfurt School social philosophers.[38] James Lindsay puts it bluntly: "grievance studies scholarship is the Bible and the Hadith of Social Justice." It is their sacred text, the ultimate authority.[39]

Let's contrast all of this to how the Bible understands authority and power.

The Bible is very clear: Ultimate authority resides with God and His revealed Word in Scripture. God also establishes legitimate human authorities: husbands in marriage, parents in the home, governing authorities in the state, and pastors and elders in the church. These authorities are to be treated with deference and respect, insofar as they adhere to godly standards of morality, because all authority comes from God.

The Bible has a *radically* different understanding of power and authority than does ideological social justice. Power and authority exist to maintain order, a necessary precondition for human flourishing, and to serve those under authority for their own benefit. God, the most powerful of all—the King of Kings and Lord of Lords—amazingly serves us by exercising His power for our good, even going so far as to die on the cross to pay the penalty for our sins—while we were His enemies!

Here's how Philippians 2:6-11 describes power and authority from the vantage point of the biblical worldview:

> [Jesus], though he was in the form of God, did not count equality with God a thing to be grasped, but

emptied himself, by taking the form of a servant, being born in the likeness of men. And being found in human form, he humbled himself by becoming obedient to the point of death, even death on a cross. Therefore God has highly exalted him and bestowed on him the name that is above every name, so that at the name of Jesus every knee should bow, in heaven and on earth and under the earth, and every tongue confess that Jesus Christ is Lord, to the glory of God the Father. (Philippians 2:6–11 ESV)

In Jesus, ultimate power and authority are combined with humility and sacrificial service. He demonstrated this throughout His early ministry. He spoke about them often, including in one particularly famous exchange with His disciples recorded in Mark 10:35–45 as they were on their way to Jerusalem. He knew what awaited Him: "The Son of Man will be delivered over to the chief priests and the scribes, and they will condemn him to death and deliver him over to the Gentiles. And they will mock him and spit on him, and flog him and kill him" (Mark 10:33–34 ESV).

The disciples were oblivious to all of this. Their expectation was that when Jesus arrived in Jerusalem, He would defeat the hated Romans and establish Himself as a powerful political ruler. They wanted power—to sit at His right and left hand (Mark 10:37) in order to "lord it over" others, and "exercise authority." We might say, they wanted to be "the boss" and throw their weight around.

Jesus takes them aside and corrects them. If they *really* want power and authority in His kingdom, this is what it means:

"Whoever would be great among you must be your servant, and whoever would be first among you must be slave of all. For even the Son of Man came not to be served but to serve, and to give his life as a ransom for many." (Mark 10:43–45)

This revolutionary biblical concept of power and authority is completely alien to ideological social justice, just as it is to every other worldview in our fallen world. For more than two thousand years, devoted followers of Jesus have attempted to follow Jesus's example in their families, places of work, and in their positions of authority in society. Wherever this culture of servant-leadership has taken root, the fruit has been utterly revolutionary.

While this kind of sacrificial servanthood also occurs, thank God, in the world outside our churches, this reality is neither acknowledged nor championed by social justice advocates. It doesn't fit their negative, zero-sum understanding of power. They don't demand power for victims so that injustices might be addressed and other people served. They seek it so that the tables can be turned on the oppressors. Jesus condemned this way of thinking when He said, "You have heard that it was said, 'An eye for an eye and a tooth for a tooth.' But I say to you, . . ." (Matthew 5:38–39a ESV).

In summary, power and authority in the Scriptures are not intrinsically negative. They are actually sources of great good when they are used to serve and benefit those under authority. They are only viewed negatively in light of human sinfulness, when they are abused for selfish, destructive ends.

And how does the Bible respond to the social justice notion that ultimate authority resides with victims? As Christians, we can agree that there are many victims of injustice and oppression in our fallen world, and they deserve justice and compassion.

However, we disagree that we must confer moral authority on people who claim victim status, allowing them to define what is real, based on their subjective "lived experience."

Take, for example, a widow whose husband was tortured and murdered in a Japanese prisoner-of-war camp in World War II. We should all agree that she is a victim. She may nurture a seething hatred of Japanese people as a result of what happened to her husband. Her "lived experience" tells her that the Japanese are inhuman barbarians. How should we respond? Do we defer to her feelings, granting her the moral authority to define what is true about Japanese people? Absolutely not. We can sympathize with her. We can understand where she's coming from, but we won't allow her to impose her "reality" on the rest us.

Christians should never allow anything other than God and the Bible to be our ultimate authority on what is true. God's Word says that all people are sinners, capable of great evil—not just the Japanese, or Jews, or white men. It also says all people are loved by God and are made in His image. The Bible, not the person who claims to be a victim, must have the final say.

As Christ-followers, we should also be concerned about the emergence of "victimhood culture." Ideological social justice drives a growing tendency to look for every opportunity to take offense and cling to every grievance, no matter how small or how long ago. This is terribly destructive. It leads to bitterness, unhappiness, and conflict. Christ shows us a very different way. Jesus calls us to turn the other cheek (Matthew 5:39) and, in genuine love, to bear all things, believe all things, hope all things, and endure all things (see 1 Corinthians 13:7). We are to "forgive one another if any of you has a grievance against someone. Forgive as the Lord forgave you" (Colossians 3:13). Rather than holding onto grievances in order to claim victim status, we are to keep "no record of wrongs" (1 Corinthians 13:5), and even to love our enemies (Matthew 5:44).

Two ways, leading to two very different cultures: forgiveness and love, or grievance and victimhood. Which kind culture do you want to create?

IS THERE A FUTURE, FINAL JUDGMENT?

The social justice worldview has no place for a final judgment. What is deemed "evil" must be rooted out here and now, by fallible men and women, using any means necessary. We've seen where this idea goes. In the former Soviet Union, "capitalists" were rounded up and shipped off to gulags or starved to death by the millions. Cambodia's Khmer Rouge had its killing fields. Red China slaughtered millions of undesirables during its horrific Cultural Revolution.

We see a similar, but not yet fully developed, dynamic in the West. Social justice power accrued through victimhood is wielded through virtual mobs on Twitter, or actual (often violent) mobs, such as those that filled the streets of nearly every Western city following the May 2020 murder of George Floyd by Minneapolis police officer Derek Chauvin. Here, you see a picture of what our society will look like if the revolution continues to dominate the culture as it already does on so many of our college campuses. No law and order. No grace. No forgiveness. No mercy. No respect for elders or teachers. No tolerance. Only screaming, aggrieved "victims" imposing vigilante justice on members of oppressor groups. It won't stay there. It isn't staying there.

Ultimately, Marxism and social justice are totalitarian, for only one human institution is seen as powerful enough to purge the world of evil and lead to utopia: an all-powerful state. Institutions that contribute to disparities—the family, church, private enterprise, and any other human association—must be expunged and replaced by an all-encompassing state. In Marxism, the state replaces God. Where the Bible says, "My God will meet all your needs according to the riches of his glory" (Philippians 4:19), Marxist social justice ideology counters: "No! *The state* will meet all your needs."[40]

This is not the Christian vision of justice. Only a perfect judge can execute perfect justice, and only Christ can perfectly fulfill that awesome responsibility. As the Judge of all, He *will* preserve all that is good while ridding the world of all that is evil.

This is the message of Jesus's parable of the wheat and the weeds (Matthew 13:24–30, 36–43). The wheat represents all that is good in the world, and the weeds represent all that is evil. "The harvest" represents the final judgment when God will separate the weeds from the wheat, burning (destroying) the weeds and preserving the wheat.

In the parable, the workers ask the owner of the field if they should go out and do the job by themselves. The owner (God), says "no" and explains that they are not capable of handling such an important job. They might uproot some wheat along with the weeds.

While rightful authorities have a duty to execute justice, even the wisest judge is fallible. On this side of Christ's return, justice will always be partial and imperfect. The job of executing perfect justice on earth is too difficult for fallen humans to undertake. In our efforts to rid the world of evil, we would destroy what is good as well. Only a perfect, holy, and righteous God is able to do this task. Only He can build the better world that all of us, in our best moments, desire. He will have the final say, but ultimate justice will have to await His return. Until that day, God extends the possibility of mercy and forgiveness to sinful people, and so do His followers, pointing to Him while we practice biblical justice along the way.

Only the biblical worldview holds out the promise of perfect justice, while also allowing for a culture marked by tolerance, grace, forgiveness, and mercy. Even in the face of great evil, we can forgive and love our enemies, trusting in God's promise to right every wrong when He returns.

CHAPTER 6

THE IDEOLOGY'S VALUES AND DISVALUES

With these building blocks in place, we can grasp how ideological social justice is no longer seen as mere personal or societal conformity to God's law. It is all about "unmasking" and overthrowing oppressive systems. And what makes these structures oppressive? They perpetuate disparities, or unequal outcomes. That word, equality, is one of the central values of ideological social justice. Core worldview presuppositions shape people's values, as well as what they despise. These, in turn, drive behavior and its real-world consequences. In this chapter, we'll look at two social justice values: equality and diversity, and two disvalues: Western civilization and America. We'll then move on to how these values lead to a wildly distorted morality and what the real-world consequences are from all this.

EQUALITY

The word "equality" has an almost sacred connotation in the worldview of ideological social justice. Equality is also a deeply biblical idea, but the social justice understanding differs greatly from what is revealed in Scripture. In the Bible, equality refers to the equality that all human beings possess as image-bearers of God. All people have equal dignity, worth, and God-given rights, though we are diverse in our sex, our personalities, our gifts, and our ethnic backgrounds. It also refers to the fact that God's law applies equally to all human beings. In the classical Marxist worldview, however, equality means equality *of outcome*—in other words, sameness, uniformity, and interchangeability. Ironically, despite its proclaimed commitment to "diversity," the actual outworking of ideological social justice is to make diverse people the same.

C. S. Lewis captures this redefinition of equality powerfully in *The Screwtape Letters*: "Let no man live who is wiser or better or more famous or even handsomer than the mass. Cut them all down to a level: all slaves, all ciphers, and all nobodies. All equals."[1] This was the goal of the communist states in the Soviet Union and China, and of all utopian experiments. People were forced to dress the same, act the same, and most importantly, *think the same*—under penalty of death if they didn't.

Social justice ideology conflates disparities (differences) with injustice and oppression. Wherever disparities exist between groups, social justice assumes that the cause *must* lie with systemic or institutional oppression of one sort or another. For example, if 80 percent of Google's software engineers are male and 20 percent are female, the disparity, *ipso facto*, *proves* systemic male privilege and sexism. Because justice equals sameness, Google must change its hiring policies.

But is this disparity *really* caused by institutional sexism? Or could men and women have different psychologies or life experiences that contribute to their being more or less inclined to become software engineers? These are dangerous questions to ask where ideological social justice holds sway. Just ask former Google software engineer James Damore, who was fired for asking them.[2]

Or consider the fact that higher percentages of black students than white students are expelled from Saint Paul, Minnesota, public schools. The superintendent, following the reasoning of social justice, has concluded that this disparity is incontrovertible proof of systemic racism.

But is it possible that the actions of the black students themselves might play a role? Social justice ideology, of course, forbids this kind of thinking. Bad outcomes must *never* be blamed on personal choices or behaviors. This is "blaming the victim"—a cardinal sin. Blame must *always* be attributed to social, systemic, and institutional causes outside of human control. So the superintendent placed an arbitrary cap on the number of black students who could be expelled, without regard to the actions of the students. The result, predictably, was "chaos."[3]

Heather MacDonald of the Manhattan Institute notes that while African Americans comprise less than a fourth of New York City's population, they account for *half* of all police pedestrian stops, a disparity that leads many to charge that the police force is institutionally racist. Not so fast, MacDonald says. "Comparing inequalities of outcome to population percentages is the wrong benchmark," she notes. "The right benchmark is crime, not population percentages. Police activity is crime-driven."[4]

She continues:

We are very reluctant to ascribe agency to blacks, or any other victim group.... The problems are all structural—white racism, white privilege, white supremacy, etc.

But this infantilizes blacks. It essentially says "there is nothing you can do for yourselves."[5]

This demand for sameness appears nearly everywhere. Norms and civic ordinances that exclude transgendered people from using the bathrooms and locker facilities of their choice are said to be unjust because they treat people differently. The laws and regulations excluding gays and lesbians from the institution of marriage must be scrapped because "same-sex" couples are to be treated the same as "opposite-sex" couples.

Not surprisingly, the mathematical equal sign, =, was the icon of the same-sex marriage movement. To argue that men and women are different and that they bring different and essential goods to marriage, procreation, and the nurturing of children violates the demand for equality or sameness. Such arguments are savagely dismissed as politically incorrect, bigoted, and homophobic. Anything that leads to unequal outcomes is suspect, according to social justice ideology.

According to John Stonestreet of the Colson Center for Christian Worldview:

> Social scientists have long known that loving families with two parents confer an enormous advantage on children. Evidence shows that these kids are more likely to attend college, less likely to suffer or perpetuate abuse, less likely to do drugs or cross the law, and have a higher likelihood of passing these advantages on to their own children.[6]

But if social justice requires equality of outcome—sameness—then loving families are unjust! Justice requires sameness. The solution? According to professors Adam Swift of the University of Warwick and Harry Brighouse of the University of Wisconsin Madison, "If the family is the source of unfairness [inequality] in society, then it looks plausible to think that if we abolished the family there would be a more level playing field."[7] This illogic is the beating heart of ideological social justice.

DIVERSITY

Along with equality, the other supreme value of ideological social justice is "diversity." The phrase "equity, diversity, and inclusion" has become a kind of mantra of the social justice movement. Countless schools, organizations, and institutions loudly champion their core commitment to equity, diversity, and inclusion. Here's one example from the University of Southern California's Price School of Public Policy, but identical language is used by any number of institutions or organizations. The language today is pervasive.

> The USC Price School Initiative on Diversity, Social Justice, and Inclusion underscores our core values of respect for differences and tolerance for all people, cultures, identities, and perspectives.
>
> . . . The initiative expands USC Price's many existing activities that engage students in promoting social justice and celebrate the richness that diversity adds to our academic community. . . . Efforts focus on [hiring] diverse faculty and staff by an inclusive approach that reaches beyond traditional advertising outlets.

Clearly, "diversity" is a central tenet of ideological social justice. The Bible also affirms diversity. But as with justice and equality, the biblical value of diversity is very different from what ideological social justice champions.

Diversity simply means difference or variety. The Bible presents diversity as a wonderful thing—but only when it is balanced by unity! God created a world of tremendous diversity. There is not one kind of flower or tree or insect or person but a great diversity of each. Of the billions of people to have walked this earth, no two are the same. God clearly loves diversity. He also loves unity. All people share a deep unity as image-bearers of God. In this most profound sense, we are all equal. We have a unity, *but not a uniformity*. Our differences as male-female, with different histories, backgrounds, families, ethnicities, languages, personalities, and gifts should be appreciated and celebrated. America's founding fathers reflected this vital unity-diversity balance in choosing our nation's motto: *E pluribus unum*, Latin for "out of many, one." America strength is found in our unity (one nation, one common culture) *and* our diversity (many ethnicities and backgrounds).

Diversity without unity is *not* a strength. It leads to chaos and conflict. Unity without diversity is also negative. It leads to stifling, totalitarian conformity. Human flourishing requires both, which is why the Bible affirms both. God's own triune nature affirms both. God is one, yet three distinct "persons"— Father, Son, and Holy Spirit.

Ideological social justice actually values uniformity, paradoxically, in the name of diversity. There is no unity-diversity balance in this worldview. The affirmation and value of "diversity" is actually strictly limited to only a few select categories. Beyond these, there is stifling pressure to conform. The diversity that is affirmed is *group* difference, not *individual* difference, and even among groups, not all group differences are equally celebrated—or even tolerated.

As we've already established, ideological social justice has no place for human beings as individuals. It reduces people to avatars or mouthpieces for the groups they belong to. They are expected to think just like everyone else in their group. If you are black, you are expected to think, speak, and act like a "black" person, and the same is true for women, LGBTQ+ people, and everyone else. There is no room to celebrate individual differences of belief inside these groups. Representative Ayanna Pressley, a black, female US congresswoman from Michigan, put words to this presupposition in comments she made at the *Netroots Nation* Conference in 2019:

> "We don't need any more brown faces that don't want to be a brown voice. We don't need black faces that don't want to be a black voice. We don't need Muslims that don't want to be a Muslim voice. We don't need queers that don't want to be a queer voice."[8]

Her point was clear. If you are brown, black, Muslim, or "queer" and you don't think or speak like your group, you are not needed. Conform to the group, or get out! There is no place in Pressley's worldview for people to think and act as individuals. This begs the question: How is the "group view" or "voice" determined? Apparently, by adherence to social justice orthodoxy. Those who fail to uphold the core doctrines of ideological social justice are denounced as traitors to their groups.

Is this a celebration of diversity? No, it is oppressive conformity.

Social justice champions speak of their "respect for differences and tolerance for all people, cultures, identities, and perspectives," but this is disingenuous. Their value of diversity isn't for "all people." For example, to proclaim that "all lives matter" is to use politically incorrect, racist language. Only some groups are celebrated, and the degree of "celebration" depends on the level of intersectional victimhood. The greater the victimhood, the greater the respect, and the greater the calls for "inclusion" in everything from college entrance policies to hiring practices to governing boards. Carl Salzman, professor of anthropology emeritus at McGill University puts it bluntly:

> Today, people are admitted to universities, to law schools, medical schools, engineering schools, hired as professors or administrators, nominated as members of Parliament, appointed ministers of the government, because of their "victim" census category, not because of competence.[9]

At the opposite end of the spectrum, the most oppressive intersectional group—straight, white males—is certainly *not* celebrated. "Inclusion" doesn't apply to it. Rather, straight, white males are expected to exclude themselves, or be excluded by others.

LGBTQ+ activist organizations, for example, are increasingly targeting Bible-believing Christians for exclusion because of their beliefs. Take the case of Christian baker Jack Philips. He has been repeatedly harassed and fined by the State of Colorado, which sought to drum him out of business for his respectful refusal to make a custom-designed cake for a same-sex wedding. For social justice activists, there certainly is no celebration of diversity, no "inclusion," no "respect for differences" or "toleration for all people and perspectives" when it comes to Philips and people like him.

A troubling example of this growing social justice–fueled intolerance—Christians (and any orthodox religious believer, Jew and Muslim alike) are being pressured to renounce their beliefs as a prerequisite for remaining in good standing in their professions or before entering the professions in the first place. Take the case of the activist group known as the Gay and Lesbian Medical Association. It developed a health-care "provider pledge" and aggressively pushed it out to medical organizations in the US. Those that fail to adopt the pledge open themselves up to charges of homophobia and bigotry. The pledge is designed to be completed by every health-care provider in the organization. It includes a number of "affirmations" with spaces next to each for employees to initial their agreement. One of these is: "I believe that lesbian, gay, bisexual, and transgender identities are within the spectrum of normal human experience and are not in themselves pathological, 'unnatural,' or sinful."

As Rod Dreher notes: "What these activists want is to make it impossible for any physician—Christian, Jewish, Muslim, or otherwise—who have any moral qualms whatsoever about anything to do with LGBT, to be driven out of the profession."[10] This is a push for exclusion. The same thing is happening in other professions.

So much for a celebration of equality, diversity, and inclusion. This is a push to get in line with the new orthodoxy *or else!* It is rank intolerance masquerading as tolerance. It is uniformity disguised as "diversity."

WHAT ABOUT THE POOR?

Perhaps you're wondering, "But what about the poor? I thought social justice was all about a concern for the poor?" Well, for much of the twentieth century, this was the case. Advocating for "the poor" working class and against its rich, capitalist, colonialist oppressors was a central feature of Marx's original economic theory, which focused entirely on class divisions.

Marx's original theory (Marxism 1.0) is based on a set of presuppositions regarding poverty and wealth that mirrors the presuppositions of ideological social justice.

- A zero-sum view of resources. "Wealth" is a material thing that exists outside of man, in banks, property holdings, and investment accounts. If some people have more, others must necessarily have less.
- Poverty is sourced in society, and particularly in unjust social arrangements and systems, such as capitalism and colonialism. It isn't sourced in fallen human hearts and false, destructive belief systems.
- The poor are helpless victims. They are not responsible for their conditions. They are unable to improve their circumstances unless other, more powerful people act on their behalf.
- It is the responsibility of government to manage and redistribute wealth and power equally among its citizens to achieve a just society.

Marx had an unshakable faith in these presuppositions. He firmly believed in the inevitability of a global communist revolution of poor, working-class victims rising against their capitalist oppressors. When that didn't pan out, a new generation of Marxist theorists de-emphasized the economic class/wealth division and highlighted other cultural divisions: between race, sex, and sexual orientation. Today, this version—Marxism 2.0—is ascendant. All the energy of the movement focuses around overthrowing the systems and structures that privilege and empower straight, white males. Certainly, concern for the poor hasn't vanished entirely in Marxism 2.0, but it is far less of a concern than during the heyday of Marxism 1.0.

In Marxism 1.0, capitalism was the enemy. How different from today, where wealthy capitalists are often some of the greatest advocates and champions of ideological social justice. It draws most of its energy and support from Western cultural elites in politics, academia, big business, and the media. Some of the most ardent backers of ideological social justice—people such as George Soros and Tim Gill—are among the wealthiest people in the world. Ideological social justice seems to have made a kind of peace with capitalism.

While concern for the poor is less of an issue for true believers in ideological social justice, Christians should remain steadfast, regardless of trends in popular culture. A concern for the poor and needy is central to Christian orthodoxy. Proverbs 19:17 (ESV) proclaims, "Whoever is generous to the poor lends to the LORD, and he will repay him for his deed," while 1 John 3:17 (ESV) warns, "But if anyone has the world's goods and sees his brother in need, yet closes his heart against him, how does God's love abide in him?" God clearly wants us to be concerned about our fellow image-bearers who are poor.

Yet our concern and our action toward the poor must be based on biblical truths about the nature of wealth and resources as well as about human nature. Namely, wealth is not fundamentally material, but spiritual, and the poor are not a class of helpless victims, but people made in God's image, with creativity, freedom, dignity, and responsibility.

- Poverty is often grounded in false, destructive beliefs. Biblical truth has the power to transform cultures of poverty.
- Wealth and resources are not "zero-sum." They are not fixed and limited but can, and do, grow and expand over time. Why? The ultimate resource isn't gold, property, or investments. It isn't material at all. It is the human mind. We are made in the image of a God who creates, and we too create (new resources, new wealth, new ideas, and so on).
- Even the poorest person has many resources that are often unappreciated but which can be transformative. A traditional Kenyan proverb says, "You can count the number of seeds in a mango but you cannot count the number of mangos in a seed." People need to be taught to see and appreciate the resources they have and their immense creative potential.[11]
- The Bible says our primary job as human beings involves governing creation[12]—properly recognizing and stewarding all that God has given us in ways that bless our families, neighbors, and nations.[13]

Yes, the poor certainly *can* be victims. They can be victims of natural disasters, wars, violence, oppressive powers, or disease, and many face dire circumstances daily in our sin-scarred world. But our view of the poor (and their view of themselves) should never be reduced to "victim." This word can describe *circumstances*, but it must never describe *identity*.

The latter consigns poor people to utter helplessness and dependence on others. It ignores key characteristics that mark our humanity: freedom, agency, responsibility, and accountability. At different times and in different circumstances, we may have more or less freedom, but even in a prison cell, we are not utterly helpless. We can still make choices about what we think, how we treat others, and so on. We need not be completely dehumanized. Good can come even from the worst of circumstances.

Silas Burgess, for example, was brought in shackles on a slave ship to Charleston, South Carolina. Orphaned at age eight, Silas later escaped to Texas with other slaves via the Underground Railroad. Eventually he owned a 102-acre farm and started the first black church and first black elementary school in his town.

Silas's great-great-grandson, Burgess Owens, is a former professional football player who is "an entrepreneur who has lived the American dream—having received a world-class education, built businesses, raised a remarkable family and, unlike most white Americans, earned a Super Bowl ring."[14] He is anything but a victim, despite his family background.

The biblical worldview also asserts that the primary job of government is to uphold the rule of law, to restrain human evil by punishing lawbreakers, and to encourage virtue.[15] It is not to equalize wealth. Doing so would necessarily violate the God-given rights and freedoms of the individual, particularly property rights established in the Ten Commandments.[16] To equalize wealth, the government would necessarily have to take (or steal) from some in order to give to others, or it would have to assume that all wealth ultimately belongs to the government.

Human flourishing doesn't come from income equality, anyway. Coveting the wealth and circumstances of others is a violation of the Ten Commandments and leads to great unhappiness. As the *Jewish Encyclopedia* says, "That covetousness is the cause of the individual's discontent and unhappiness is certainly true."[17] True happiness is found in taking responsibility for my life and providing for the needs of others. This action affirms my human nature and dignity and leads to deep contentment.

Ideological social justice and biblical Christianity, as two distinct and irreconcilable worldviews, have two very different ways of "seeing" poverty and impoverished people. These two sets of assumptions lead to two different approaches to working with the poor and two different outcomes. Tragically, in the name of social justice, many Christ-followers have mistakenly affirmed the first set of nonbiblical assumptions when they should champion the second. There are many things we can and must do to help the poor. But our actions ought to be based on biblical truths about the nature of human beings, wealth, and resources.[18]

Basing our actions on the faulty Marxist assumptions that frame so much of the social justice discussion of poverty will only harm those we are seeking to help. Regardless of our motives, treating the poor as helpless victims and taking away their agency and personal responsibility—essentially treating them as livestock—is one of the most destructive and dehumanizing things that we could ever do.

WESTERN CIVILIZATION AND AMERICA

The complex web of white, male, heteronormative structural oppression and domination that people like Ta-Nehisi Coates (and many others) rail against was woven, social justice proponents say, over many generations. How we came to our present lamentable state is essentially the story of Western civilization—a civilization whose defining characteristics are slavery, colonization, greed, exploitation, racial superiority, imperialism, and genocide.

For the millions who have been taught this neo-Marxist narrative of Western history since the 1960s, "The West" is nothing more than "a mythos of white power, imbibed by white supremacists."[19] Speaking for many, a student activist at Claremont Pomona University charges that Western civilization has given rise to "interlocking systems of domination that produce lethal conditions under which oppressed peoples are forced to live."[20] These systems include a toxic brew of capitalism, "whiteness," traditional marriage ("the patriarchy"), the male-female binary, and Judeo-Christian sexual morality. All are oppressive. All have to be thrown into the trash heap of history.

The loathing of Western civilization carries over to America as well. According to the influential historian Howard Zinn, author of *A People's History of the United States*, the American Revolution was nothing more than an effort by wealthy white men to protect their privileges.

> The inferior position of blacks, the exclusion of Indians from the new society, the establishment of supremacy for the rich and powerful in the new nation—all this was already settled in the colonies by the time of the

Revolution. With the English out of the way, it could now be put on paper, solidified, regularized, made legitimate, by the Constitution of the United States, drafted at a convention of Revolutionary leaders in Philadelphia.[21]

Speaking of America, Coates chimes in with his assertion that America is fundamentally and irredeemably racist: "White supremacy is not merely the work of hotheaded demagogues, or a matter of false consciousness, but a force so fundamental to America that it is difficult to imagine the country without it."[22] For the many who think like Coates, America is "an awful, no-good, very-bad, racist country that we ought to despise, tear down, and remake."

This loathing of Western civilization and America is behind two recent trends: athletes not standing for the National Anthem and refusing to honor the American flag, and the desecration and tearing-down of statues, murals, and portraits that commemorate famous historical figures such as George Washington, Winston Churchill, and Christopher Columbus. For social justice ideologues, these icons of Western civilization and American history are not heroes but villains who perpetuated systems of violence, oppression, and bigotry.

Incidentally, if you claim to be a conservative, social justice advocates will assume that what you want to "conserve" are the very oppressive systems that have advantaged white, straight males at the expense of everyone else. In short, to be a conservative *is* to be a patriarchal, homophobic, white supremacist. No wonder politics in America has become so toxic and divisive as ideological social justice has expanded its influence.

While there is much for which the West can be criticized—including race-based slavery, the Salem witch trials, an oft-greedy focus on material goods, and the Spanish Inquisition just for starters—Christians are called to take a far more nuanced view of Western civilization and American history, both the good and the bad. Our perspective needs to be focused on finding truth, not confined to a narrative that cherry-picks and spotlights only the negative.

Although John Winthrop held out hope that the new land would be a "city upon a hill,"[23] the truth is, America is not the New Jerusalem. "The claim is not that the West is and has always been a perfect paradise of justice and equality," Bo Winegard says. "It is not and it has never been. But, whatever its flaws, it has raised more people out of indigence, misery, superstition, and intolerance than any other civilization in history. Today, it is laudably cosmopolitan and largely free from grotesque forms of discrimination and bigotry."[24]

For all its flaws, Western civilization offers so much that is good—freedom of conscience, freedom of speech, freedom of religion, respect for the individual, due process, relative peace and prosperity, and so on. These goods arose from an understanding of biblical truth lived out imperfectly, but faithfully, over many generations. Those attacking the West are doing so, largely, with the tools provided by the civilization itself. The social justice narrative ignores this history entirely. We ought not to.

When evaluating the West, it's important to recognize that we are not dealing with a single, monolithic culture. It's actually two quite different cultures that share a common history and geography. Western culture divided during the period between the Reformation and the Enlightenment.

Following the lead of Enlightenment rationalists and atheistic philosophers, one stream abandoned God and gave rise to the secularization of society. Among its fruits were the French and Russian revolutions. Today, this stream underpins postmodernism, Marxism (old and new), and ideological social justice. The other stream emerged from the German Reformation. It affirmed the Judeo-Christian roots of the West and asserted the authority of God over all of life and all of society. This stream fed into the English and American revolutions. It is still influencing churches and nations around the world, even though it has been eclipsed by the secular stream in Europe and North America. It was this stream that supplied the nutrients that gave rise to the freedoms, tolerance, respect for the individual, the rule of law, due process, and prosperity that the West has enjoyed.

So when talking about "the West" or Western civilization, or American history, both streams must be taken into account. Both streams, for example, have shaped free-market capitalism. So capitalism isn't one thing, but two very different things. Whether capitalism, on the whole, is good or bad for society depends on *which* capitalism you are looking at.

A secularized capitalism devoid of Christian virtue and objective morality is rapacious, greed-centered, and an engine for the spread of all kinds of evil, including pornography, abortion, and prostitution. But the capitalism that continues to be influenced by the Reformation—and the authority of God, objective morality, and virtue—is an engine of godly stewardship, generosity, prosperity, and blessing. Both forms of capitalism are with us today. The same can be said about "freedom," "law," or "the American dream." The West is now, essentially, two separate cultures at war with one another.

Yet many people fail to make this distinction, including many leading evangelical leaders. They are quick to criticize

Western civilization, capitalism, or the American dream,[25] or even America's legacy of freedom,[26] as if these were all one thing. *They are not.* As Christians, our problem isn't with "Western civilization" but with the *secularization* of Western civilization. While "the West" is not synonymous with Christianity, the Judeo-Christian roots of the West (and of America) need to be recognized, celebrated, and preserved. Our task, as Christians, shouldn't be to tear down the West, but to reform it to better reflect the truth of God's kingdom.

As Christians, we are called to be a humble, grateful people. We should have an attitude of humility toward our forebears. The attitude that only criticizes the past reveals a haughty pride that essentially says, "We would have been more virtuous and courageous if we had lived in their times and in their circumstances." This kind of historical arrogance has no place in the heart of a Christian. Rather, we should recognize that just like our predecessors, we are flawed people, and show them the same grace we would want extended to us for our shortcomings. We should also be aware of and grateful for our inheritance. The *many* good things that we too easily take for granted have come to us over the course of Western and American history, through people who labored to preserve and pass along powerful, biblical ideas that are good, true, and beautiful, often at great personal cost. Their memory deserves to be honored. Not because they were perfect, but because they gave us a great gift of a relatively free, just society. We should never cease to be grateful for what they entrusted to us.

This kind of gratitude and humility toward the past is completely absent from adherents of ideological social justice. By choosing to feed a critical spirit, focusing only on the negative, they convince themselves that there is very little, if anything, to be grateful for and much to despise. (It is not called "critical theory" for nothing!) But a haughty, critical spirit that willfully ignores all the good gifts that other have given you, often a great expense—is a terrible thing. It destroys relationships, and the relationships we have with our forebears are among our most important.

A DISTORTED MORALITY

So where do the core worldview presuppositions and the values and disvalues of ideological social justice lead? To a wildly distorted, upside-down morality.

Ideological social justice is a highly moral movement. Some have even described the movement as "puritanical."[27] It has a finely defined sense of right and wrong, and its followers relish the righteousness and moral purity the ideology affords them.

What does this "morality" look like? It certainly doesn't involve what historically were considered virtues—things like honesty, kindness, chastity, patience, forgiveness, marital fidelity, modesty, or civility. No, it means one thing: overturning oppressive systems and liberating marginalized groups.

The movement is also very aggressive in its efforts to impose its morality on others. It obsesses over maintaining a sense of moral purity, not only within its own ranks, but also imposing it on everyone else, not only through social media shaming and mobbing, but increasingly by leveraging private and public authorities to impose rules and regulations and to levy punishments on evildoers.

This is seen, perhaps, most clearly in the new sexual morality promulgated by ideological social justice, which says, you are immoral if you

- insist that the male, female binary is a fact—a biological reality;
- assert that marriage is a lifelong covenant between a man and a woman;
- believe that sex should be reserved for marriage; and
- fail to affirm and celebrate homosexuality, lesbianism, transgenderism, or any other sexual identity.

Abortion plays a central role in this moral system. For its adherents, abortion isn't a necessary evil that should be "safe, legal, and rare," but a positive moral good and a fundamental human right. Abortion, at any time, for any reason, is a matter of social justice—*reproductive* justice. There is no thought given to the life of the unborn. They are ignored or dehumanized.

On matters of race, the distorted morality of ideological social justice follows the contours of intersectionality. If you are part of the oppressor group, expect your transgressions to be highlighted. Even the slightest offense or "microaggression" will be "called out" and held against you. If you are a member of a victim group, your transgressions (and the victims of your transgressions) will be largely ignored.

In Chicago, much was rightly made of the 2014 shooting of Laquan McDonald, a seventeen-year-old African American, by a white police officer, who eventually was convicted of second-degree murder in 2018.[28] While the McDonald incident reshaped the city's politics and sparked numerous demonstrations, the city's horrific ongoing murder rate—with most of the victims being African American[29]—gets little press. Why? Because the vast majority of these murders are committed by blacks against other blacks. In the worldview of ideological social justice, to even mention this fact is insensitive and racist. Blacks are victims; therefore, the violence they perpetuate is largely ignored by the media. Try and speak out for the victims of black-on-black crime, and you'll find yourself quickly called out, corrected, or shamed.

Around the world, girls and women face gendercide, rape, trafficking, acid thrown in their faces, and murder simply because of their sex.[30] Yet their plight is mostly ignored by social justice activists in the West and by a compliant media. Why? Because the perpetrators have victim group status as Muslims or other non-Western, former colonies. Here's a cardinal rule of social justice morality: Victim group members can never be portrayed as perpetrators of injustice. They are and must always remain victims.

While they ignore gross injustices against women and girls in countries like Somalia or Pakistan, these same social justice activists will nearly hyperventilate when they perceive the slightest "injustice" against women in the West—for example, when birth control is not paid for by their insurance plans. Said one pediatrician arguing against a federal decision to no longer force employers with religious or moral objections to pay for contraception, "This isn't just about women's health. We have a right to have sex."[31]

Even as social justice ideology elevates "micro" injustices beyond all sense of proportion, it ignores or downplays major injustices. Abortion, the most serious injustice of our generation, has legally eliminated more than 60 million unborn human beings since 1973. Yet it is widely held to be a positive moral good.

For some, trying to uphold such a distorted, upside-down morality is too much to bear. Frederica Mathewes-Green was a young pro-choice feminist. But after reading a physician's account in *Esquire* of an abortion, her eyes were opened. "There I was, anti-war, anti–capital punishment, even vegetarian, and a firm believer that social justice cannot be won at the cost of violence," Mathewes-Green recounted. "Well, this sure looked like violence. How had I agreed to make this hideous act the centerpiece of my feminism?"[32]

This perplexing state of affairs poses real challenges for Christians. Will we go along with the warped and distorted social justice morality, or will we have the courage to speak out on real injustices where they exist, such as abortion, black-on-black violence, or female gendercide? Will we adopt the distorted moral priorities (and blinders) of ideological social justice, or will we allow the Bible to guide us on matters of justice and morality?

- Will we adhere to biblical sexual morality or seek to compromise with the sexual revolution?
- Will we commit ourselves to the fight to end the most grievous injustice of our generation—abortion—or will we remain on the sidelines, silent and ambivalent?
- Will we ignore injustices perpetrated by members of victim groups, or will we judge impartially, regardless of where the perpetrators fit on the intersectional spectrum?
- Will we speak out for victims of injustice, regardless of skin color, ethnicity, stage of life, or sex? Will *all lives* matter or only those from self-defined victim groups?

God's own character and revealed Word define the difference between good and evil. His law is authoritative on matters of morality, particularly the Ten Commandments. Our commitment must be to this law, and not to societal moral norms, no matter how popular they are or how high a price we may have to pay for violating those norms.

Unfortunately, there is growing temptation among some evangelicals to soft-pedal or dismiss Old Testament law as irrelevant. Andy Stanley, the pastor of North Point Ministries in Atlanta, has called on Christians to "unhitch" themselves from the Old Testament, saying, "Participants in the new covenant are expected to obey the single command Jesus issued as part of his new covenant: as I have loved you, so you must love one another." Stanley adds that this new commandment is "a replacement for everything in the existing list. Including the big ten."[33]

This is wrong! As the Lord said in the Sermon on the Mount, He came not to abolish the law, but to fulfill it (Matthew 5:17)! Not a single word of the law will be left unfulfilled. Stanley's statements reflect the worst kind of antinomian theology. If we do not uphold God's moral standards—His law—who will? And if we lose God's law, the only alternative is man-centered morality, which is subjective and changeable, depending on who has power.

Another growing temptation, particularly concerning issues of sexuality, comes when we replace biblical sexual morality with a more therapeutic, feelings-centric approach, in some cases going so far as to claim that God's law is unloving and uncompassionate. Such thinking has deeply compromised the Episcopal Church. For example, the Episcopal Church in the Diocese of Washington, DC, passed a resolution in 2018 to no longer use masculine pronouns for God in updates to its Book of Common Prayer. The resolution urged the church "to utilize expansive language for God from the rich sources of feminine, masculine, and non-binary imagery for God found in Scripture and tradition and, when possible, to avoid the use of gendered pronouns for God." The drafters explained,

"By expanding our language for God, we will expand our image of God and the nature of God."[34]

Some of us, meanwhile, succumb to the lie that "God made me like this," whether the person is trans, gay, or whatever. And if "God made" them this way, then it must be okay to act on it. Remember all the talk about a "gay gene"? It doesn't exist! As the American Psychological Association says, "No findings have emerged that permit scientists to conclude that sexual orientation is determined by any particular factor or factors. Many think that nature and nurture both play complex roles."[35]

But even if the Almighty did allow such feelings and besetting sins, the Bible never says it's okay to let them control us. Rather, we are to be transformed by the renewing of our minds (Romans 12:2) and think about "whatever is true, whatever is honorable, whatever is just, whatever is pure, whatever is lovely, whatever is commendable" (Philippians 4:8 ESV) and choose to do right.

WHAT IS LOST?

What do we lose if ideological social justice continues to eclipse the Judeo-Christian belief system as the primary shaper of our common culture? We are already seeing change and can expect to see much more:

- Less gratitude and more grievance
- Less personal responsibility and more claims of victim-hood, hostility, division, and blame casting
- Continued erosion of the rule of law, with moral norms and laws becoming arbitrary, constantly changing, conforming to the whims of whatever group can marshal power to sway popular opinion

- The loss of due process; no more "innocent until proven guilty"
- The loss of free speech; no more ability to debate and discuss challenging topics openly (By shutting down debate, the door opens ever wider to violent extremism.)
- The loss of truth and the rise of a pervasive culture of narrative creation and perpetuation in the service of amassing ever-greater power and control
- The erosion of religious liberty (Our first freedom is increasingly framed as a cover for bigotry and a weapon for oppressing so-called "sexual minorities.")
- The loss of the gospel (Social justice ideology is utterly incompatible with the Christian gospel. It offers a false righteousness for victim-group members and a false form of atonement for oppressors. As such, it is a false gospel—and one that ultimately has no room for forgiveness, reconciliation, or redemption, only ever-greater division, condescension, and retribution.)
- The loss of any basis for civility, social unity, cohesion, or tolerance; no more "live and let live"; no more "love your enemy"
- No hope of future justice (Evil must be purged in the present through twitter mobs and protest marches, but it won't stop there. If we don't alter our course, the evil will have to be rooted out through gulags, guillotines, or death camps.)

GIBSON'S BAKERY V. OBERLIN COLLEGE: A WINDOW TO THE FUTURE

What will society look like if ideological social justice becomes the established "cult" in Western culture—the underlying religious belief system that shapes our collective values and disvalues and drives our choices, actions, policies, and laws? We might look to any number of growing instances and examples, but here I'll focus on one in particular that I believe provides a clear window into what awaits us.

The story, according to Tom Gibson, owner of the family bakery began at Gibson's Bakery in Oberlin, Ohio, in the fall of 2016:

> We own and operate Gibson's Bakery in the city of Oberlin, Ohio—home to Oberlin College. [For more than 130 years, our family has] worked hard to build a reputation on our homemade baked goods, candy and ice cream, and on our commitment to our community. . . .
>
> The bakery has long been a popular stop among students, residents and returning alumni. Our family and business' reputation was a source of pride for generations. But all that changed . . . on November 9, 2016, [when] a student attempted to shoplift two bottles of wine from our store. . . .
>
> Police arrested the student. But the next day, hundreds of people gathered in protest. From bullhorns they called for a boycott. The sidewalk and park across the street from our store were filled with protesters holding signs labeling us racists and white supremacists.

The arrest, they said, was the result of racial profiling. The narrative was set and there was no combating it.

Despite the lack of any evidence, our family was accused of a long history of racism and discrimination. Oberlin College officials ordered the suspension of the more than one-hundred-year business relationship with our bakery, and our customers dwindled. We were officially on trial—not in a courtroom, but in the court of public opinion. And we were losing.

As time went on, the truth began to emerge. The shoplifter confessed to his crime and said the arrest wasn't racially motivated. But Oberlin College refused to help set the record straight by issuing a public statement that our family is not racist and does not have a history of racial profiling or discrimination.

The damage had been done. And the truth seemed irrelevant. In a small city like Oberlin, having the largest business and employer against you is more than enough to seal your fate.

Running out of options, we decided to pursue a lawsuit against Oberlin College. Two regional law firms agreed to take our case.

What few understand is that this situation not only affected our business; it also touched every aspect of our lives.

In the end, the words of my father inspired me to continue the fight. He said, "In my life, I've done everything I could to treat all people with dignity and respect. And now, nearing the end of my life, I'm going to die being labeled as a racist."

There wasn't enough time, he feared, to set the record straight. His legacy had been tarnished and he felt powerless to stop it. I had to see this case through.

This experience has taught me that reputations are a fragile thing. They take a lifetime to build but only moments to destroy. . . . In an age where social media can spread lies at an alarming rate, what happened to Gibson's Bakery could happen to anyone."[36]

Notice how ideological social justice presuppositions played out in this parable:

- Truth, facts, and evidence don't matter. "The truth seemed irrelevant," says Gibson. "Despite the lack of any evidence, our family was accused of a long history of racism and discrimination."
- Narrative replaces truth. "The narrative was set, there was no recasting it."
- Following the logic of intersectionality, the perpetrator (a person of color) was cast as the victim, and the victim (Gibson, a white man) was cast as the villain.
- Mob justice, shaming, and intimidation were utilized. "Hundreds of people gathered in protest. From bullhorns they called for a boycott. The sidewalk and park across the street from our store were filled with protesters holding signs labeling us racists and white supremacists. . . . We were officially on trial—not in a courtroom, but in the court of public opinion."
- Institutional backing supported the mob: "Oberlin College refused to help set the record straight by issuing

a public statement that our family is not racist and does not have a history of racial profiling or discrimination."

In this story, the so-called victim is a person of color, but it could just as easily be a woman or a sexual minority. The same dynamics come into play. The same basic script is followed. Recall the 2018 confirmation of Supreme Court Justice Brett Kavanagh. At the last possible moment, a woman, Christine Blasey Ford, accused Kavanagh of raping her. No evidence was found to back up her claim, but it didn't matter. Social justice ideologues ran to her defense with the refrain: "We must always believe the victim!" They were backed up by screaming, hysterical mobs, which, in turn, were backed up by multiple institutions and organizations, all intent on destroying Kavanagh's reputation by any means necessary.

These stories show very clearly what social justice looks like in practice. By now it should be clear that there is no relationship between ideological social justice and biblical justice. They are utterly distinct in their presuppositions, values, and outcomes. Christians do us no favors when they liken biblical justice to social justice, as one prominent evangelical leader recently did:

> "Biblical justice includes all forms of God-ordained justice, including . . . social justice."[37]

Such people apparently fail to see how social justice is the accepted label for a fully formed worldview—one utterly opposed to the biblical worldview and its conception of justice. The fact that "social justice" is now the brand associated with a virulently anti-Christian worldview must be seen for what it is: a form of satanic deception. We shouldn't be surprised by this. Satan "disguises himself as an angel of light" (2 Corinthians 11:14 ESV), often by cloaking his destructive purposes in biblical words and language. Christians must see through this. I'm not advocating that we abandon the word "justice." That is ground we can never cede; it is indeed our "home turf." But it is folly to confuse biblical justice and *social justice*. It is only sowing confusion when the need of the hour is clarity.

HOW WILL WE RESPOND?

How will followers of Jesus Christ, who are commissioned to disciple the nations (Matthew 28:18–20), working for the blessing of our neighbors and society, respond to all this? Will we sit on the sidelines and keep our heads down as this new ideology washes over our nations? Worse, will we intentionally or unintentionally support a destructive ideology in the name of fighting for justice? Or will we commit to upholding biblical truth rather than this hostile ideology, out of love for our neighbors and even our enemies?

We need careful discernment and wise choices.

CHAPTER 7

INROADS INTO THE CULTURE . . . AND THE CHURCH

Ideological social justice has been incredibly successful at penetrating and shaping the broader culture and at warp speed. It is the reigning ideology in nearly every major metropolitan area. Its presuppositions dominate huge swathes of the culture, particularly in these areas:

- The academy, and particularly in the humanities, social sciences, departments of education, and university administration, as well as public K–12 education
- Mainstream media and entertainment
- The progressive wing of the Democratic Party
- Big tech and Silicon Valley, including powerful companies such as Google, Apple, Facebook, Amazon, and Twitter
- The boardrooms and human resource departments of major corporations and associations, where the mantra "diversity, equity, and inclusion" has become pervasive

- Professional credentialing and accrediting organizations in education, law, medicine, and more
- Mainstream Protestant denominations, such as the Episcopal Church, the United Church of Christ, and the Presbyterian Church (USA)

Because of the outsized influence of these institutions, all of us have absorbed, at some level, the assumptions and values of ideological social justice in ways we are likely unaware of. And yet there remain large swathes of the culture that remain steadfastly opposed to ideological social justice, including:

- Rural and blue-collar communities
- The majority of Bible-believing, church-attending evangelicals, as well as a significant number of Catholic and Orthodox Christians and Orthodox Jews
- The conservative wing of the Republican Party
- A small but vocal group of academics, public figures, and YouTube celebrities, including Jordan Peterson, Jonathan Haidt, Camille Paglia, and others

THE RESPONSE OF THE EVANGELICAL CHURCH

Evangelicalism appears to be fracturing in response to ideological social justice, with many or most prominent leaders, universities, and organizations moving toward implicitly or explicitly endorsing ideological social justice.

Whenever a hostile, nonbiblical worldview gains widespread influence in a culture, pressure is exerted on the Bible-believing church. Historically, the church responds in one of three ways:

- It *conforms* itself to the reigning ideology by jettisoning orthodox biblical teaching in an attempt to align itself to the core presuppositions of the emerging ideology. This is typically motivated out of a desire for self-preservation. The belief is that unless we conform to the reigning worldview, the church will be marginalized and weakened.

- It *accommodates* the reigning ideology, often unintentionally. The new ideology changes culture so rapidly that it washes over Christians without their full awareness and begins to infiltrate their thinking. There isn't necessarily a conscious choice to abandon orthodox Christianity, but over time, as one assumption after another of the new ideology is embraced, biblical orthodoxy slowly erodes.

- It *resists* the reigning ideology. It sees the threat with open eyes and responds by holding fast to orthodox biblical teaching, no matter the cost. In many cases, resistance leads Christians to disengage from the broader culture, particularly when it comes to educating their children. Resistance leads to open confrontation with the broader culture.

We saw this play out in Germany in the 1920s and '30s with the rise of National Socialism. Eric Metaxas's masterful book *Bonhoeffer: Pastor, Martyr, Prophet, Spy* tells how Nazi ideology splintered the church in Germany. Tragically, the majority of churches and Christian institutions conformed or accommodated themselves to the new ideology. Some even went so far as displaying the swastika from church pulpits. The "Confessing

Church" resisted, openly confronted Nazism, and ultimately paid the price for this choice with their lives. The church in Germany has yet to recover from these cataclysmic events.

We saw this play out in the United States in the late 1800s and early 1900s, when an aggressively secular ideology, fueled by Darwin's naturalistic theory of evolution, began to sweep through the academy and into the broader culture.

Some mainstream Protestant denominations chose the path of conformity. Their secularized version of Christianity replaced the historic gospel with the "social gospel." Accordingly, man wasn't fallen, but perfectible. The problem with society wasn't human sinfulness, but social inequality. The solution wasn't inward spiritual regeneration, but external government programs designed to reengineer society in order to eliminate social inequities. Horace Greeley (1811–1872), founder and editor of the *New York Tribune*, succinctly summarized the social gospel this way:

> The heart of man is not depraved . . . his passions do not prompt to wrong doing, and do not therefore by their actions, produce evil. Evil flows only from social [inequality]. Give [people] full scope, free play, a perfect and complete development, and universal happiness must be the result. . . . Create a new form of Society in which this shall be possible . . . then you will have the perfect Society; then you will have the Kingdom of Heaven.[1]

For many other Christians, however, this kind of talk was utterly heretical. Rather than conforming to the rapidly advancing secular ideology, these Christians chose to resist. They became known as "the fundamentalists" and were led by people such as J. Gresham Machen and R. A. Torrey. They held fast to basic biblical doctrines such as the authority of the Bible, the fallen nature of mankind, the reality of a future judgment, and the atonement.

The resulting bitter conflict between mainstream Protestantism and fundamentalism fractured the Western church. In its weakened condition, the church lost much of its societal influence, and the emerging secular ideology increasingly filled the cultural vacuum. Once-orthodox institutions, including nearly all of the Ivy League universities, abandoned biblical Christianity and rapidly secularized.

The fundamentalist movement of the early 1900s gave rise to present-day evangelicalism. Their resistance preserved the gospel and biblical orthodoxy in America, and today, the Bible-believing church remains a significant cultural force. And while we rightly honor them for their courageous stand, they made one significant error. In reacting against the social gospel, they abandoned historic Christian teaching on Christian engagement in society. In doing so, they replaced a biblical worldview with a form of Gnostic dualism that separated reality in "higher" and "lower" categories. The higher concerned itself with things of the spirit, heaven, evangelism, and church ministry. The lower (and less important) encompassed almost everything else, including nearly all forms of cultural engagement. This was increasingly viewed by fundamentalists as not only futile but unbiblical. "Culture" was conflated with an irredeemably fallen world. God wasn't concerned with changing the culture, but rescuing people. In *Modern Revivalism: From Charles Grandison Finney to Billy Graham*, this William McLoughlin quote of Dwight L. Moody captures the mindset perfectly: "I look upon this world as a wrecked vessel. God has given me a lifeboat and said to me, 'Moody, save all you can.'"[2]

In their unfortunate reaction against the social gospel, the fundamentalists downplayed clear biblical teaching on the responsibility of the church to be salt and light in culture, and to love our neighbors, particularly the impoverished and marginalized. The storied legacy of Christian social engagement, stretching back to the work of the early church in the ancient Roman world, to the great works of the heroes of the modern Protestant mission movement such as Amy Carmichael, William Wilberforce, and William Carey, was largely ignored and forgotten. Lost was the biblical approach to ministry that seamlessly links evangelism and discipleship to matters of justice and social transformation.

Take, for example, Amy Carmichael (1867–1951), one of the most respected missionaries of the first half of the twentieth century. She had no problem engaging the culture. Among her other works, Carmichael established a ministry to protect, shelter, and educate temple prostitutes in India. In the later years of her ministry, new missionaries from the West came out to India and began to challenge Carmichael, claiming that her efforts to fight the injustice of temple prostitution in India were "worldly activities" that distracted her from the "saving of souls." To this, she simply replied, "Souls are more or less firmly attached to bodies."[3]

Fast-forward to 2010. Yet again, an aggressive and unbiblical ideology, a toxic stew of postmodernism and neo-Marxism that for years had incubated in Western universities, began to influence the broader culture. The church, once again, began to fracture in response. This time, however, the split wasn't between the fundamentalists and mainstream Protestantism. The split was (and is) within evangelicalism itself.

THE CONFORMING COALITION

On one side of the divide are those who, intentionally or un-intentionally, have chosen the path of conformity. This faction has been referred to variously as "the evangelical left" or "Progressive Christianity." Their early leaders included Jim Wallis, founder of *Sojourners* magazine and Ron Sider of Evangelicals for Social Action, as well as progressive Christian leaders such as Brian McLaren, Rob Bell, and Rachel Held Evans.

Early leaders focused primarily on issues of poverty and economic inequality. For the newer leaders, "justice" wasn't limited to the economic realm. Following the lead of cultural trendsetters, justice involved standing up for the whole intersectional array of oppressed groups: women, the LGBTQ community, and racial minorities or "people of color."

Women

The rise of ideological social justice in the universities during the 1950s and '60s parallels the rise of second-wave feminism. In 1963, Betty Friedan published *The Feminine Mystique*, and Gloria Steinem launched *Ms.* magazine. Their feminist movement championed the full equality of men and women, with "equality" defined as sameness or interchangeability. Second-wave feminism found a home in universities. The 1980s witnessed a rapid rise of Women's Studies programs and majors.

For second-wave feminists, sexual equality meant getting women out of the home and into the workforce. They associated domestic life with servile oppression. The biblical notion of male headship in the home—disparaged as "the patriarchy"—was anathema. Men were increasingly viewed as sexual predators and rapists. Masculinity was increasingly described as "toxic."

The patriarchy was nothing more than a hegemonic, oppressive structure—the ultimate source of inequality, injustice, and oppression. For second-wave feminists, the introduction of the birth control pill in 1960, along with legalized abortion in 1973, were heralded as great triumphs of female liberation. Pregnancy and the nurture of infants and children, which had been seen as hindrances to full equality with males, were finally overcome.

Starting in the 1980s a faction of evangelicals began to align with second-wave feminism, bringing its basic presuppositions into the church under the banner of "egalitarianism." In 2016, *Relevant* magazine proclaimed, "Evangelical feminism is on the rise, and the conversation is getting loud enough for the most traditional churches to hear."[4]

That conversation was led by a new generation of evangelical leaders who more or less echoed the ideas and language of second-wave feminism, with a thin Christian veneer. For scholar, activist, and minister Monica Coleman, the central issue was power: "Feminism in religion is about voice and power. . . . Where are the women in the story? Who has voice? Who doesn't? . . . Who is in leadership in churches? Whose voices and perspectives have the loudest voice and influence?"[5]

This reduction of human relationships to power dynamics is, of course, part and parcel of ideological social justice. Others, such as the late evangelical feminist blogger and speaker Rachel Held Evans, spoke out against the evils of patriarchy. "Patriarchy is not God's dream for the world. Those who continue to perpetuate it perpetuate an injustice, which of course harms the Church internally and also its witness to the watching world."[6]

Today, these ideas have become mainstream within evangelicalism. The idea of male leadership in the home and church is increasingly viewed as outdated and oppressive. Evangelicals who hold to a "complementarian" view increasingly find that they are a minority in churches, Christian schools, and organizations.

LGBTQ+

The gay rights movement (later extended to the LGBTQ+ movement) is one of the most stunning examples of cultural transformation in American history. In the blink of an eye, views on sexuality, marriage, and family that held sway in the West for millennia were upended. As recently as 1996, only 27 percent of the US population supported same-sex marriage. By 2013, support for same-sex marriage had jumped to 53 percent. Today it is even higher, with 73 percent support among the millennial generation.

This moral upheaval didn't happen by accident. It was the result of a carefully crafted strategy, the basic blueprint of which was provided in 1989 by Marshall Kirk and Hunter Madsen in their highly influential book *After the Ball: How America Will Conquer Its Fear and Hatred of Gays in the '90s.*[7] The strategy had four overarching goals: (1) change the flamboyant, sexually addicted stereotype of gays by portraying them as normal Americans who are a significant minority in every community; (2) make homosexuality a matter of biological determinism, not moral choice; (3) portray opponents of homosexual behavior as hateful bigots who should be stigmatized, silenced, and equated with Jim Crow racists; and (4) portray LGBTQ rights as the new civil rights, with members of the LGBTQ community portrayed as the victims.

Over the next twenty-five years, every one of these goals was achieved. LGBTQ activists cleverly focused on the arts, entertainment, and celebrity culture. At the 2003 MTV music video awards ceremony, two of the most popular entertainers at the time, Madonna and Britney Spears, helped to normalize homosexuality by passionately kissing onstage.

The 2005 film *Brokeback Mountain* won multiple Oscars for "courageously" teaching that neither marriage, the needs of children, nor commitment should stand in the way of homosexual passion. A year later saw the launch of *Will and Grace*, a hugely popular ten-season sitcom that significantly destigmatized homosexual life. In 2009, another sitcom, *Modern Family*, began its ten-season run, depicting a wholesome, suburban same-sex couple raising children. In 2012, the comedy-drama *Glee* did its part to normalize the homosexual lifestyle. It ran for six seasons and 121 episodes.

By the early 1990s, the changes in sexual morality began to impact the professions and, ultimately, to be codified into laws. In 1993 the American Psychological Association removed homosexuality from its catalog of mental disorders. Ten years later, in *Lawrence v. Texas*, the Supreme Court ruled that states could not legislate against intimate behavior between consenting adults. And then, in 2004, Massachusetts became the first state to legalize same-sex marriage. Eventually, thirty-six more states would follow, leading to the landmark 2015 Supreme Court ruling, *Obergefell v. Hodges*. Today, same-sex marriage is the law of the land.

The speed and force of this moral revolution put enormous pressure on the church. To uphold historic biblical teaching on sexuality, family, marriage, and even the male-female binary branded you a retrograde, narrow-minded bigot. Christian businesses and institutions came under increasing pressure to conform to the new sexual orthodoxy or face a variety of penalties. The leaders of the LGBTQ moral revolution made it clear that their goal was not coexistence but total victory. And they are winning. Here again, we see the zero-sum view of power held by true believers in ideological social justice. There can be no win-win. Peaceful coexistence isn't possible.

As we've seen over and over, this kind of strong, organized cultural opposition places enormous pressure on the Bible-believing church. In 2016, David Gushee, a prominent American evangelical university professor and former columnist for *Christianity Today*, issued a warning to his fellow evangelicals. Either get on board the LGBTQ rights movement or face even more dire consequences.

> You are either for full and unequivocal social and legal equality for LGBT people, or you are against it, and your answer will at some point be revealed. This is true both for individuals and for institutions. Neutrality is not an option. Neither is polite half-acceptance. Nor is avoiding the subject. Hide as you might, the issue will come and find you.
>
> Openly discriminatory religious schools and parachurch organizations [that is, those that uphold the historic, biblical sexual ethic] will feel the pinch first. Any entity that requires government accreditation or touches government dollars will be in the immediate line of fire. Some organizations will face the choice either to abandon [historic biblical sexual morality] or risk potential closure. Others will simply face increasing social marginalization.[8]

According to columnist Rod Dreher, "Gushee has fully embraced gay rights, and doesn't simply tolerate gay relationships, but affirms their goodness."[9] He's not alone. According to Pew Research, by 2016, 51 percent of millennial evangelicals expressed support for same-sex marriage; 54 percent said homosexuality should be accepted and encouraged, not discouraged. These younger evangelicals increasingly see the LGBTQ community within the framework of ideological social justice, as a marginalized, oppressed community. The oppressors are those that uphold a biblical view of marriage and sexuality. To love one's LGBTQ neighbor means accepting their views on sexuality and their calls for full "marriage equality."

Rachel Held Evans walked away from the evangelical church over these issues. She wrote, "I explained that when our gay, lesbian, bisexual, and transgender friends aren't welcome at the table, then we don't feel welcome either, and that not every young adult gets married or has children, so we need to stop building our churches around categories and start building them around people."[10] Who doesn't want to be "welcoming"?

Race

Race, more than any other issue, is leading evangelicals into the arms of ideological social justice. In the years following the subprime economic collapse of 2007–10, a new generation of evangelical leaders came to the fore championing antiracism and speaking out against "whiteness" and "white privilege." Their emergence paralleled a number of events that rocked the culture, including the 2012 shooting of Trayvon Martin in Florida, the rise of the #BlackLivesMatter movement in 2013, and the race riots in Ferguson, Missouri, in the wake of the fatal shooting of Michael Brown one year later.

Racism is a great and ever-present evil. As followers of Jesus, we are duty bound to fight it, in all its terrible forms. Likely all Christians agree on this. Here's the problem: we no longer have agreement about what racism is. Some say it is "prejudice plus power" which only applies to white people by virtue of their monopoly on cultural power. Others hold to the definition found in Merriam Webster's Dictionary: "The belief that race is the primary determinant of human traits and capacities and that racial differences produce an inherent superiority of a particular race."[11]

These are very different definitions. If you hold to the first, white people are, by definition, racist oppressors because of the unearned privileges they possess based on their supposed cultural power. To deny this only proves unconscious racism. It can only be acknowledged, confessed, and lamented.

If you hold to the second definition of racism, then the first definition is, itself, racist. It lumps people together based on their skin color and problematizes them, implying they are all stained with the guilt of racism whether they know it or not. Douglas Murray describes this as "antiracist racism."[12] This definition, rooted in critical race theory and "whiteness studies," exacerbates racial hostility by judging millions of people based on their outward appearance.

These two definitions are part of two larger, conflicting narratives about race in America. Understanding these narratives is key to understanding the highly charged racial climate we find ourselves in. Both narratives have roots in the black community. Both have historic and present-day black champions.

THE REVOLUTIONARY NARRATIVE

Let's examine the outlines of these two narratives. I'll call one the *Revolutionary Narrative*. It holds that existing social, cultural, and economic systems and institutions are so corrupted by racism that there is no possibility for reform. They need to be torn out, root and branch, to make way for a new order.

The Revolutionary Narrative flows out of the presuppositions of ideological social justice. It is, without question, the dominant race narrative in America today. It is taught exclusively in our public schools and universities, aggressively promoted through social and legacy media, entertainment, big business, and increasingly, through our evangelical churches and institutions.

Historically, versions of the Revolutionary Narrative were championed by the likes of W. E. B. Du Bois, James Baldwin, Elijah Muhammad, Malcolm X, and James H. Cone. Contemporary popularizers include Michelle Alexander, author of *The New Jim Crow*; *Atlantic* essayist Ta-Nehisi Coates; popular critical race theorists such as Robin DiAngelo, author of *White Fragility*, Barbara Applebaum, author of *Being White, Being Good*, and Ibram X. Kendi, author of *How to Be An Antiracist*; Louis Farrakhan, political activist and leader of the Nation of Islam, and Black Lives Matter founders Alicia Garza, Opal Tometi, and Patrisse Cullors, to name just a few.

Here, in broad outline, is my summary of the Revolutionary Narrative:

- Systemic injustice and institutional racism must be emphasized. The problems that black people face are sourced outside their community, in the larger society, and have attributed to historic slavery and pervasive, systemic white oppression.

- For positive change to happen in the black community, white people need to change. They need to own up to their "whiteness," confess their complicity in systemic oppression, transfer power and resources to black people, and not defend themselves, which only makes problems worse by demonstrating their "white fragility."

- The biggest problems facing the black community are near-genocidal levels of police brutality and a systemically racist criminal justice system. The criminal justice system is "The New Jim Crow," as demonstrated by the fact that black people are arrested and imprisoned at far higher rates than white people in comparison to their percentage of the overall population.

- America, from its very origins, is a fundamentally racist nation. Indeed, the very essence of America is not freedom but oppression. Essayist Andrew Sullivan puts it this way: "All the ideals about individual liberty, religious freedom, limited government, and the equality of all human beings are a falsehood to cover for, justify and entrench the enslavement of human beings under the fiction of race."[13] Ultimately, the only way change can happen is for these systems to be unmasked, deconstructed, and dismantled.

- "Color-blind" is a racist sentiment. Those who use this phrase merely demonstrate their insensitivity to the oppression, violence, and discrimination that black people face. We need to be more aware of our skin color, not less—more aware of the way that race divides us, not less.

- Racism resides almost entirely on the political right. The Republican Party is deeply stained by xenophobia, bigotry, and white supremacy, while the Democratic

Party stands for civil rights. "Democrats have a long and proud history of defending civil rights and expanding opportunity for all Americans [including support for] the Civil Rights Act of 1964."[14]

- #BlackLivesMatter—and its advocacy against rampant police brutality—is the most important civil rights movement in America today.

THE PRESERVATION NARRATIVE

While the Revolutionary Narrative dominates our racial discourse today, another narrative exists that doesn't get nearly as much attention. Far fewer people are aware of its broad outline or its most prominent advocates. I'll call it the *Preservation Narrative*. It affirms the goodness of America's founding principles and seeks to preserve them while desiring to continually improve our systems and institutions to more perfectly reflect these principles.

Like the Revolutionary Narrative, the Preservation Narrative has deep roots in the black community. Historically, forms of it were championed by people like Frederick Douglass, Booker T. Washington, George Washington Carver, Jackie Robinson, and Jessie Owens. It is perhaps most movingly expressed in Martin Luther King Jr.'s famous "I Have a Dream" speech.

Today, its most fervent advocates are black. They include Supreme Court Justice Clarence Thomas, former presidential advisor Robert Woodson, economists Thomas Sowell and Walter Williams, conservative author Shelby Steele, former Secretary of State Condoleezza Rice, Vanderbilt political science professor Carol Swain, South Carolina Senator Tim Scott, neurosurgeon Ben Carson, author and activist Alveda King, radio personality Larry

Elder, Wall Street Journal columnist Jason Riley, cultural critic Candace Owens, entertainer Kanye West, Harvard economist and author Glenn Loury, and pro-life activist Ryan Bomberger, to name a few.

Here, in broad outline, is my summary of the Preservation Narrative:

- Personal choice and responsibility must be emphasized, and evil must be seen as first rooted in human hearts and minds before manifesting in society. While white racism persists, it is far from the biggest challenge facing the black community. The challenges in the black community can be overcome in ways that are not dependent on the actions of white people, but the choices and actions of black people themselves.

- The biggest challenges facing the black community today include the following: (1) The devastation of the black family—The out-of-wedlock birth rate in the black community went from 35 percent in 1970 to 72 percent today.[15] This has led to several generations of fatherless, alienated young black men who turn to gangs and criminal activity. (2) Abortion— since the 1973 Roe v. Wade Supreme Court ruling, 19 million black babies were aborted in the US[16]. (3) Educational systems—Far too many young black people are trapped in failing schools and given no access to other options that would improve their educational opportunities.

- The devastation of the black family is largely attributable to the rise of the modern welfare state. Black economists Walter Williams and Thomas Sowell argue that the significant expansion of federal welfare under the

Great Society programs beginning in the 1960s have contributed to the destruction of African American families. According to Sowell, "The black family, which had survived centuries of slavery and discrimination, began rapidly disintegrating in the liberal welfare state that subsidized unwed pregnancy and changed welfare from an emergency rescue to a way of life."[17]

- America has a tragic history of racial oppression and slavery. Yet our founding principles in the Declaration of Independence ("all men are created equal and are endowed by their Creator with certain unalienable rights") led to the eventual eradication of slavery and to significant progress in racial equality. Today, America is one of the least racist countries in the world and a land of opportunity for people of all ethnic backgrounds, which is why immigrants continue to flock here in huge numbers, including many with black and brown skin.

- "Color-blind" is a cultural achievement to be celebrated, for it frees us from the scourge of tribalism. Rather than generalizing about people based on skin color, "color-blind" means that I see people first and foremost as unique individuals and free moral agents. This was Martin Luther King Jr.'s famous dream—that his children would not be judged by the color of their skin, but the content of their character.

- Historically, racism in America was perpetuated primarily by those on the political left. The Democratic Party defended slavery, started the Civil War, opposed Reconstruction, founded the Ku Klux Klan, imposed segregation, perpetrated lynching, and fought against the civil rights acts of the 1950s and '60s.

- #BlackLivesMatter is a radical, neo-Marxist revolutionary organization that exists to exacerbate racial tensions as a means of fomenting social, cultural, and economic revolution.

EVALUATING THE TWO NARRATIVES

Like all narratives, truth can be found in both. *But this is not to say that they are both equally true.* How do we as Christians respond to these two narratives?

The first instinct of many sincere Christians when presented with these two alternative views of race in America is to remain neutral—or to try to find a middle ground. Many white Christians, out of a righteous desire to build relationships with to those in the black community, end up supporting the Revolutionary Narrative as part of the process.

Both of these motives are understandable and well-intentioned. But as Christians, our primary obligation is to the truth and to love. That means we have to evaluate narratives carefully. We need to affirm what is good and true and reject what is false and destructive.

In my ongoing examination of these narratives, I believe the Preservation Narrative is far more truthful and will result in far better outcomes for the black community. I recognize that many Christians of good conscience will strongly disagree with me, and I welcome any opportunity to dialogue, to be challenged, and to learn. Here are the issues I have considered and how I have come to my conclusions:

Human nature

The Revolutionary Narrative is rooted in victimology. It's basic message to black Americans is this: No matter how hard you try, you are set up for failure because a vast array of racist structures and systems are working against you. It's message to white Americans is this: By virtue of your skin color, you are guilty of benefiting from these same systems whether you realize it or not. It's a disheartening message to blacks and a guilt-inducing message to whites, one that only exacerbates racial tensions. Personally, I believe that any narrative that invites people to nurture grievances toward people with a different skin color is a horrible narrative.

The basic message of the Preservation Narrative is far more truthful with regard to human nature. It says, in the words of essayist Andrew Sullivan, "No racial group is homogeneous, and every individual has agency. No one is entirely a victim or entirely privileged." [18]

The Preservation Narrative says to young black people: In America today, if you graduate from high school, hold almost any job, and wait until you are married to have children, you will be well on the road to a fruitful, flourishing life—and you can make these choices no matter what white people do or don't do. This is an empowering and unifying message.

Police brutality

The Revolutionary Narrative uses catastrophic, hyperbolic language to describe police brutality. It's most influential advocates routinely malign the police as "killers"[19] who "hunt down"[20] black people and are perpetuating "genocide"[21] against them.

The police—like all fallen human beings—are far from perfect. There are bad cops, and when they commit violent criminal acts, all people of good conscience, including most police, demand that they be held to account. There is widespread agreement on these points. But this is not enough for advocates of the Revolutionary Narrative. To them, the problem isn't with particular cops; the police system as a whole is poisoned with institutional racism.

A vast amount of data regarding police use of violent force against black people allow us to examine the veracity of this claim, and it turns out that the evidence doesn't support the charge. In 2019, according to the Washington Post database of police shootings, in a nation of 330 million people, a total of fourteen unarmed black Americans were fatally shot by police.[22] And these were not innocent bystanders. Most were attacking police officers at the time they were shot.

Don't misunderstand me, fourteen lives lost to police brutality is fourteen too many. Each life is precious beyond measure. But this is hardly evidence of systemic police racism, must less a genocide. The reality today is that a police officer is far more likely to be killed by a black male than an unarmed black male is to be killed by a police officer.[23]

Yet tragically, the myth that the police themselves are a threat to black people has taken deep roots inside the black community. Many sincerely believe it. Every interaction they have with the police is viewed through this prism. As a result, a deep-seated fear and mistrust now exists between many in the black community and the police. This itself is a problem that needs to be addressed. Christians should be empathetic to the experiences black people have with the police. We should listen and try to understand, but we should also not perpetuate a myth. Affirming false beliefs is never a loving thing to do.

The criminal justice system

The Revolutionary Narrative indicts the criminal justice system as a whole as structurally racist. It bases this on the fact that more black people are arrested, charged, and convicted than white people when compared to their percentage of the overall population. But this analysis is flawed and deceptive. It completely ignores the relatively high crime rates in the black community that drive higher levels of arrest and incarceration. Black Americans commit serious violent crime at rates over three times their representation in the general population. For example, although blacks constitute 12 percent of the population, they consistently commit over one-half of all homicides.

It wasn't always this way. In the 1950s, blacks committed fewer crimes than whites based on their percentage of the population. Blacks also had lower out-of-wedlock birth rates than whites.[24] The rise of crime in the black community parallels the breakdown of the black family starting in the 1960s and '70s. Crime rates rise as the capacity to self-govern erodes. This is a truism that applies to people of any skin color. Self-government doesn't come naturally. It has to be inculcated, and the primary institutions that do this are the family, the church, and the school. Since the 1960s, all three of these institutions have eroded in the black community—particularly the family and schools. To truly help black lives, this has to be reversed. According to the Preservation Narrative, these vital institutions that impart virtuous self-government need to be strengthened.

Abortion

The biggest source, by far, of violent death in the black community is abortion. If there is a "genocide," then abortion is it. The most influential advocates of the Revolutionary Narrative ignore this, and in fact, demand the expansion of the legalized murder of black children. This alone should prevent Christians from supporting it.

The United States

As Christians, our approach to history has to be based on truth. We must allow history to guide us. We cannot manipulate and distort it to further a particular agenda. To focus exclusively on one aspect of history—either the good or the bad—is to perpetuate a lie.

Unsurprisingly, the Revolutionary Narrative, as typified by the *New York Times*'s 1619 Project does just that. According to that narrative, the US was founded upon principles that exist to perpetuate white, male supremacy. It is known primarily for its systemic white racism, slavery, greed, patriarchal oppression of women, and the genocidal treatment of native peoples. This kind of manipulation of history is typical of many revolutionary movements, but it is a despicable tactic.

The Preservation Narrative also focuses attention on America's tragic history of racial oppression and slavery, but also focuses on what is good, thus telling a far more truthful story. It teaches that our founding principles in the Declaration of Independence made the eventual eradication of slavery possible. While racism and slavery are common among all nations in human history, what makes America unique is our response to these evils. We ended slavery and have made tremendous progress in addressing overt racism, eliminating barriers to equal opportunity, and recognizing the racial sensibilities of minorities.

There are many parts of our history that we should teach our children to be proud of. Yet the Revolutionary Narrative either whitewashes the good out of the history books or downplays them. Here are some examples of things we can celebrate:

- The world's first organized antislavery society was formed in Pennsylvania in 1774.
- The first legal ban on slavery anywhere in the world was in Vermont in 1777.
- Five of the original thirteen states followed suit either during or immediately after the Revolution, passing bans on slavery between 1780 and 1784.
- The first federal ban on slavery, in the Northwest Territory, was drafted in 1784 by Thomas Jefferson and passed by the Confederation Congress in 1787. Its language would later be adopted directly into the Thirteenth Amendment.
- Congress banned the slave trade at the first possible moment, in 1807, at the insistence of President Jefferson.
- Slavery was eventually abolished after a bloody civil war in which many thousands of white people died to end this evil institution.
- Significant progress in racial equality was made through the Civil Rights movement of the 1950s and '60s.
- We elected the first black president in 2009, and he served for two terms. The country celebrated this milestone, including those who didn't vote for Barack Obama because of his policy positions.

If systemic white oppression is woven into the very fabric of America, Andrew Sullivan wonders how to account for

> the historic growth of a black middle and upper class, increasing gains for black women in education and the workplace, a revered two-term black president, a thriving black intelligentsia, successful black mayors and governors and members of Congress, and popular and high culture strongly defined by the African-American experience? [What is to account for the fact that] nonwhite immigrants are fast catching up with whites in income and . . . some minority groups now outearn whites?[25]

Racism on the left and the right

The Revolutionary Narrative popularizers place the blame for the perpetuation of white supremacy almost entirely with those on the political right. This is almost entirely false. Consider these facts:

- The Republican Party was founded in 1854 as an antislavery party. Its mission was to stop the spread of slavery into the new western territories with the aim of abolishing it entirely.
- In the infamous Dred Scott v. Sandford Supreme Court case, the court ruled that slaves aren't citizens; they're property. The seven justices who voted in favor of slavery were all Democrats. The two justices who dissented with both Republicans.
- During the era of Reconstruction, hundreds of black men were elected to southern state legislatures as

Republicans, and twenty-two black Republicans served in the US Congress by 1900. The Democrats did not elect a black man to Congress until 1935.

- After Reconstruction, it was southern Democrats that enacted laws that restricted the ability of blacks to own property and run businesses. And they imposed poll taxes and literacy tests, used to subvert the black citizen's right to vote.
- The Ku Klux Klan was founded by a Democrat, Nathan Bedford Forrest.
- President Woodrow Wilson, a Democrat, was deeply racist. He resegregated many federal agencies and supported eugenics policies that targeted blacks.
- Margaret Sanger, a far-left progressive, was a racist eugenicist and founder of Planned Parenthood. Her birth control and later abortion movement has led to the death of more black lives in America than were killed during slavery.
- Jesse Owens, a staunch Republican, won four gold medals at the 1936 Berlin Olympics, he was snubbed by Democratic President Franklin Roosevelt. Roosevelt only invited white Olympians to the White House.
- The only serious congressional opposition to the Civil Rights Act of 1964 came from Democrats. Eighty percent of Republicans in Congress supported the bill. Democratic senators filibustered the bill for seventy-five days.

Why then, do overwhelming numbers of black people support the Democratic Party today? Advocates for the Preservation

Narrative have a straightforward answer: massive government welfare programs have resulted in a debilitating dependence on the government for millions of black Americans. Democrats support these programs, so a vote for the Democratic Party is a vote to keep the money flowing.

My aim here isn't to indict Christians who support the Democratic Party. I know many and respect them. I do want to challenge the prevailing narrative on this topic.

#BlackLivesMatter

As Christians, we of course agree that black lives matter. At the same time, we have to recognize that the organization that goes by this name is very discriminating in its advocacy for black lives. It turns out that, for them, only a highly select few matter—namely victims of white police brutality. When it comes to *the following* black lives, the Black Lives Matter organization is utterly silent:

- The millions of innocent black lives snuffed out through legalized abortion
- The horrific number of blacks killed, day in and day out, as a result of inner-city and gang-related violence
- The many black police officers killed in the line of duty
- The many black children consigned to failing schools, with no choice to better their educational opportunities

Given this, shouldn't we question whether the organization, Black Lives Matter, truly cares about black lives? It isn't hard to get accurate information on what they stand for. It only takes a few minutes to review their website—blacklivesmatter.com— and look at their main funding sources. There is no doubt that they are a far-left revolutionary front group that cynically *uses* racial tensions to further its revolutionary agenda. Here are a few things it openly advocates for:

- The abolition of the family—mothers and fathers— replaced by a form of communalism where children are raised collectively—This is the same basic policy that all Marxist regimes advocate.
- A society that is "queer affirming" and the expansion of LGBTQ+ rights
- The expansion of abortion "services" in the black community
- The abolition of free-market capitalism, replaced by a form of Marxist collectivism
- The defunding of the police

Yet many Christians of good conscience support Black Lives Matter campaigns, marches, and protests out of a desire to stand in solidarity with black people and speak out against racism. They should take time to look at what they are supporting, what's behind the organization's very clever (and devious) marketing and branding.

Christians who wish to truly see flourishing in the lives and communities of their black brothers and sisters should consider supporting groups that work to strengthen black families, strengthen black businesses, advocate for school choice, and fight against the scourge of abortion in the black community— groups like the Woodson Center (www.WoodsonCenter.org); the Radiance Foundation (www.TheRadianceFoundation.org); or the American Federation for Children, a school choice advocacy organization (www.FederationForChildren.org).

These groups, and many others like them, get virtually no attention in the mainstream media, and very little on social media. Unlike Black Lives Matter, they have no multimillion-dollar publicity budget funded by far-left billionaires and foundations like George Soros and the Tides Foundation. They don't receive glowing endorsements from vast numbers of major corporations, sports associations, and celebrities, as Black Lives Matter does. The empowered solutions they advance deserve the support of the Christian community far more than Black Lives Matter does.

Tactics

The highly aggressive advocates of the Revolutionary Narrative employ tactics very similar to those used in the past by Marxist revolutionaries. They treat their narrative as sacrosanct. You cannot do or say anything that calls it into question, and woe to the one who tries. And if you choose to not advocate for it—that too will be viewed as complicity in racism.

Anyone who dissents from the narrative can expect to be denounced as a racist and summarily bullied, shamed, intimidated, threatened, or fired. Advocates of the Revolutionary Narrative have little interest in engaging in free, open debate. They want submissive compliance. The bending of the knee is a perfect symbolic expression for the Revolutionary Narrative as a whole.

As Christ-followers, we should have nothing to do with these despicable bullying and intimidation tactics, and we shouldn't support those who use them. They are eerily reminiscent of Mao's Cultural Revolution. We must remain a people committed to civility, respect, and free and open debate and dialogue in the pursuit of truth.

WOKE CHURCH

The most passionate black advocates of the Revolutionary Narrative, past and the present, are either non-Christians or nominal Christians. By contrast, the vast majority of black advocates for the Preservation Narrative are deeply committed Christians. Given this, it is a grievous irony to see so many prominent evangelical leaders and organizations lending their support to furthering the Revolutionary Narrative. A good example is pastor Eric Mason, author of the 2018 book *Woke Church: An Urgent Call for Christians in America to Confront Racism and Injustice.*

Mason is an impressive figure. He is the African American founder and pastor of Epiphany Fellowship in Philadelphia, where he is active in church planting and various worthy inner-city ministries. He earned his Master of Theology from Dallas Theological Seminary, and his PhD from Gordon Conwell Theological Seminary. His book received endorsements from such evangelical luminaries as John Perkins, Ligon Duncan, and Tony Evans.

In reading Mason's book, I found many places where I deeply resonated with his teaching and his heart. In many places, he was solidly biblical and, surprisingly given his book's title, affirmed much of the unwoke Preservation Narrative. For example, he:

- affirmed a color-blind way of thinking: "We should feel more at home with the people in the Christian family than our own ethnicity. . . . It grieves my heart to see that we so often treat each other like we're from different bloodlines."[26] "My dream is that we lock arms together as true brothers and sisters. . . . We need to look at each other and say, 'You're family.'"[27]

- expressed a passion for the gospel as the cutting edge of social change: "Jesus is still the answer for the world today. I'm praying that God will cause our souls to turn to Him. . . . We need Him to help us, first of all, not forget the gospel. We need Him to help us not forget the centrality of Jesus, the might of the cross, and the power of the resurrection to save and transform souls".[28]
- emphasized responsibility and Christlike service: "We must be known for our obedience and our readiness to do good to others. We must not be contentious. We must be gentle, courteous people. . . . It starts with character. . . . We must reach into the community and serve the needs of others".[29]
- desires to move beyond virtue-signaling and make a difference: "The Woke Church is one that is aware of the urgent needs in the community and does more than just talk about those needs. It marshals its forces to make a difference."[30] This led his church to be involved in teaching biblically based sex education.
- emphasized education: "Our young people are our greatest treasure and responsibility. Every one of them should have a quality education."[31]
- emphasized family: "The family is the foundation of our communities. . . . The church needs to be a family training center."[32]

But in his teaching on racial issues, he mostly repeated talking points of the Revolutionary Narrative, often contradicting what he expressed in other parts of the book. For example, he:

- regularly employed the lexicon of the Revolutionary Narrative, such as, "structural oppression" and "privilege."[33]
- explained to his son that "his people" were not so much fellow Christians, or fellow Americans, but people with black skin.[34]
- suggested that encounters with the police are the most dangerous circumstances that young black men in America face.[35]
- worried that if blacks and white Christians were to worship together in the same congregation, that whites would "find a way to subjugate blacks and make us dependent on them."[36]
- provided a list of things Christians ought to lament, yet somehow, the millions of unborn black children violently aborted since 1972 didn't make his list.
- disparaged the concept of "color-blindness" suggesting that it is anti-Christian.[37]
- engaged in the hyperbole common among advocates of the Revolutionary Narrative, saying that in America today, "black lives are systematically and intentionally targeted for demise," and that blacks face "deadly oppression." He does not back up these claims by evidence.[38]
- praised the Black Lives Matter organization as "a voice of black dignity" and wished that the church had founded this movement, but made no effort to explain the Marxist roots of the organization or the deeply unbiblical policies it supports.[39]
- portrayed America's history in a uniformly negative light by focusing on the ways that slavery and systemic racism

continue to influence the lives of black Americans, yet never expressed gratitude for the incredible progress that America has made in overcoming slavery or racial discrimination.

- endorsed the views of W. E. B. Du Bois,[40] and sited popularizers of the Revolutionary Narrative like Michelle Alexander,[41] yet never mentioned black heroes like George Washington Carver, a deeply committed Christian, or any other historic black supporters of the Preservation Narrative.

Mason is a prominent evangelical leader with seemingly one foot in historic, biblical Christianity and the other in ideological social justice, and he is far from alone. The list of important evangelical leaders, pastors, and organizations following this same course is long and growing.[42] And these leaders are influencing the emerging generation of young pastors. In one difficult conversation I had with a pastor in his thirties from an influential evangelical church in Arizona, he pleaded with me to confess my complicity in racism due to "the power and privileges that I have and have always had, because I am a white man."

The church isn't supposed to blindly follow mainstream cultural trends—even powerful ones with massive elite support and financial backing. It is supposed to uphold and live out the counter-cultural ways of Christ's kingdom as salt and light in the midst of an increasingly dark and chaotic culture. Unless the church pulls its foot out of the ideological social justice quagmire, and places both feet firmly on the solid ground of biblical truth, the consequences will be devastating for both the church and the nations we exist to bless and serve.

THE BITTER FRUIT OF CONFORMING: DECONSTRUCTING FAITH

Whether by default or intention, the attempt to combine biblical theology with the presuppositions of ideological social justice is leading to heartbreak. Neil Shenvi's admonition is worth repeating: Biblical Christianity and ideological social justice are *incompatible* worldviews. They are diametrically opposed on matters of epistemology, human nature and identity, morality, and authority.

Eric Mason is refreshingly honest about his own struggles with this tension, which he first became aware of in seminary. In *Woke Church*, he writes about the growing divide between his white fellow students, who were more interested in gospel proclamation and conversion and skeptical of the "social gospel."

> Initially, I didn't understand [the social gospel], but after studying James H. Cone [an influential black liberation theologian], I came to understand what this meant. I found myself exegetically at home with my conservative family on the doctrines of grace, but ethically at home with my liberal family on issues of race and justice.

He continues:

> My theological home of conservative Christianity has become more confusing as the years have gone on. . . . In many ways I have one foot in conservative Christianity and the other in liberal Christianity.[43]

The "liberal Christianity" that Mason is drawn to—whether it's the mainstream variety found in the Episcopal Church or the United Church of Christ or the newer "Progressive Christianity"—is fully conformed to ideological social justice in its embrace of LGBTQ+ rights, abortion, third-wave feminism, and critical race theory.

No wonder Mason's confusion is growing. He's attempting to live with two incompatible worldviews. This will almost certainly prove to be unsustainable. In all likelihood, one will lose out to the other. For most, like the late Rachel Held Evans, her Christian faith lost out, as it did with a growing number of well-known millennial evangelical pastors and teachers like Rob Bell, Bart Campolo, and Josh Harris.

Our increasingly postmodern culture tells us that *we*—not the Holy Scriptures—are the supreme authority. We determine what is true and good, including what is true and good in the Bible itself. On top of this, our young evangelicals are taught in countless ways that America, a supposedly "Christian nation," is oppressive, genocidal, and patriarchal. In a recent survey, two thirds of millennials believed that America is a racist and sexist country, and close to 40 percent think the United States is "among the most unequal societies in the world."[44]

Is it any wonder that so many young Christians are "deconstructing" their faith? Bart Campolo, son of well-known evangelical teacher Tony Campolo, admitted that moving toward theologically liberal views was "the beginning of the end" of his faith:

> I passed through every stage of heresy. It starts with sovereignty going, then biblical authority goes, then I'm a universalist, now I'm marrying gay people. Pretty soon I don't actually believe Jesus actually rose from the dead in a bodily way."[45]

WHY ARE SO MANY CONFORMING?

There can be no doubt that ideological social justice has made rapid, deep inroads into the very heart of American evangelicalism. Outspoken advocates of critical race theory and ideological social justice teach in our evangelical universities and seminaries, have their books published by our most prominent publishing houses, and their articles published by deeply respected institutions like *Christianity Today* and *The Gospel Coalition*. They have been given platforms to share their message with huge numbers of young evangelicals by groups like InterVarsity and Cru (formerly Campus Crusade for Christ).

While these evangelical institutions and organizations continue to affirm historic statements of faith and doctrine, they simultaneously validate the presuppositions of ideological social justice by adopting its language and endorsing its core presuppositions. Why are so many influential evangelical teachers and organizations supporting a clearly unbiblical ideology? There are several possible reasons.

First, there is the deceptive "Trojan horse" element of this ideology. On the surface, it champions things all Christians stand for: justice, racial equality, the dignity of women, and love toward those in the LGBTQ+ community. Many Christians embrace ideological social justice because they see it as the next great civil rights movement.

To give these Christian leaders the benefit of the doubt, I'm sure they want to do the right thing. They want to show compassion for those who are hurting. They want to "mourn with those who mourn." They look at the victims of injustice and see image-bearers of God, and they long for justice to prevail. So they join forces with deeply unbiblical organizations and movements that appear to be biblical on the surface, in their talk of social justice, equality, and the value and dignity of "black lives." But below this benign surface is an ideology that is incompatible and profoundly hostile to historic Christianity.

Far too many well-intentioned Christians are falling into this trap.

Then there is the immense social pressure that comes with not affirming ideological social justice. Its advocates claim that unless you fully accept their worldview presuppositions, you are not simply wrong, you are evil—a racist, sexist, patriarchal bigot. The price that cultural gatekeepers are demanding to remain in their good graces is full, unquestioned acceptance of their ideology. Tragically, many evangelicals appear willing to pay that price.

Owen Strachan, associate professor of Christian theology at Midwestern Baptist Theological Seminary, spoke powerfully against this temptation:

> In recent decades, evangelicals have thirsted after cultural approval. Like the world's saddest pageant contestants, we want desperately to be accepted by secular culture. We have exchanged our holy birthright for a Facebook fan page. Our hermeneutic is not motivated by righteous awe, by fear and trembling, by the honor and magnificence of our God. It is driven by a craven desire to be liked, to be culturally acceptable, to be *au courant*. . . . The church should not be a preening wannabe. It should recognize . . . that it is a counterculture. We are the city of God, the true city.[46]

But perhaps the deepest reason that evangelical leaders are embracing ideological social justice goes back to the great rupture of American Christendom at the beginning of the twentieth century when both mainstream Protestantism and fundamentalism abandoned the biblical worldview, replacing it respectively with either the social gospel or with a form of Gnostic dualism.

What was lost on both sides? The historic, biblical understanding of justice and cultural engagement. That rich heritage was neglected and nearly forgotten.

And so today many evangelical leaders who are passionate for justice and social change have little knowledge of a fully formed biblical worldview, including a biblical view of justice. They were never taught it, nor were their forebears. You have to go back generations—to Amy Carmichael, William Wilberforce, and William Carey and a time when the Bible-believing church viewed its mission as a seamless linkage of gospel proclamation, discipleship, and social and cultural impact.

This has left many evangelical leaders in a vulnerable position. With little understanding of the original (biblical justice), far too many have fallen for the counterfeit (ideological social justice). As a result, they find themselves syncretized to a false religion, one that works against the very thing they purport to champion—genuine justice.

THE RESISTANCE COALITION

While social justice is the reigning ideology among cultural gatekeepers in the West, it has some influential critics. Perhaps the most well-known group has been dubbed "the intellectual dark web." They include Jordan Peterson, University of Toronto psychology professor; Jonathan Haidt, a social psychologist at New York University; and Camille Paglia, feminist academic and social critic. This highly diverse group includes liberals, conservatives, orthodox Jews, gays, and lesbians. What unites them is a common set of values that run counter to ideological social justice. These include commitments to the following:

- Reason, logic, civil debate, and free and open inquiry in the pursuit of truth
- Freedom of speech, association, and religion
- Civility, respect for ideological opponents, and a "live and let live" ethic of tolerance
- Western (and American) values and traditions
- The individual, including the importance of moral choice, character, and responsibility
- On matters of race, a commitment to the credo of Martin Luther King Jr.: We judge each other on the basis of "the content of our character, not the color of our skin."

While these values are consistent with a biblical worldview, noticeably absent are any prominent evangelicals. Instead of making common cause with these non-Christian opponents of ideological social justice, many evangelical leaders have opted to remain neutral, or even worse, to implicitly or explicitly support it.

But there are exceptions. A relatively small but influential group of evangelicals has organized an effort to resist the encroachment of ideological social justice into the Bible-believing church. These include John MacArthur, pastor of Grace Community Church and chancellor of The Master's University in Santa Clarita, California; theologian and pastor Douglas Wilson; Tom Ascol, president of Founders Ministries and pastor at Grace Baptist Church in Florida; and Voddie Baucham, dean of theology at African Christian University in Zambia. In 2018, these men came together to issue their "Statement on Social Justice and the Gospel."

> We are deeply concerned that values borrowed from secular culture are currently undermining Scripture in the areas of race and ethnicity, manhood and womanhood, and human sexuality. The Bible's teaching on each of these subjects is being challenged under the broad and somewhat nebulous rubric of concern for "social justice." . . . It is our earnest prayer that our brothers and sisters will stand firm on the gospel and avoid being blown to and fro by every cultural trend that seeks to move the Church of Christ off course.[47]

This is an important and much-needed warning. There is tremendous confusion within evangelicalism on these subjects. This confusion needs to be replaced by a careful discernment of the fundamental differences between biblical justice and this new social justice pseudo-religion. John MacArthur puts it this way: "Those who let the culture, a political ideology, popular opinion, or any other extrabiblical source define 'justice' for them will soon find that Scripture opposes them. If they are determined to retain a perverted idea of justice, they will therefore have to oppose Scripture."[48]

If the yeast of ideological social justice continues to shape evangelical theology and practice, the church will be greatly hindered at a time when the culture desperately needs to see true, biblical justice advocated and lived out.

Yet while there is much to affirm in the Statement on Social Justice and the Gospel, it unfortunately repeats the same error of the earlier fundamentalist movement. Rather than reasserting the rich legacy of biblical social engagement, the statement drifts into the old sacred-secular dichotomy that pits gospel proclamation against social ministry.

> We emphatically deny that lectures on social issues (or activism aimed at reshaping the wider culture) are as vital to the life and health of the church as the preaching of the gospel and the exposition of Scripture. Historically, such things tend to become distractions that inevitably lead to departures from the gospel.[49]

Let's be specific. "Social issues" and "social activism" include the pro-life movement, efforts to uplift the poor, the addicted, and the broken, and the fight against sex trafficking. Are these activities a "distraction" from the mission of the church? Are they somehow competing against the preaching of the gospel?

Phil Johnson, a close associate of John MacArthur, has said that for evangelicals to engage in the culture on issues of life, poverty, justice, and human dignity is "mission drift." They are "a distraction" from the central mission of the church—gospel proclamation.[50]

Rather than calling the church back to an orthodox, biblical approach to justice and cultural engagement, Johnson and others are falling into the same error as the earlier fundamentalists. Rather than defending Christian social engagement, with its seamless, biblical relationship between gospel proclamation and cultural transformation, they are calling into question the very validity of Christian cultural engagement and justice ministry.

The problem with fundamentalism it was that it was defined largely by what it was against—the social gospel and theological liberalism. In reacting against the social gospel, it abandoned "social" ministry of any kind. It threw the baby out with the bathwater. This meant that the secular culture alone was able to define what social and cultural engagement was, and how it should be done, for more than a generation.

The reactionary approach was wrong then, and it is wrong today.

The crying need today, as it was in the early twentieth century, is to recover a biblical, orthodox approach to justice and cultural engagement. *At the same time, we must speak out against unbiblical social justice ideology.* We need to rediscover and champion a deeply biblical approach to cultural engagement, in ways that lead to greater justice and human flourishing, and not to abandon these things as a distraction from our "core mission."

In short, the church must return to a comprehensive biblical worldview. Biblical justice is far too important, and far too central to the Christian worldview, for us to allow it to be compromised by an imposter such as social justice.

The fundamentalists, and those evangelicals reacting today against ideological social justice, may think they are upholding biblical orthodoxy, but in fact they are promoting a quasi-biblical worldview that divides the world into a sacred-secular dichotomy. Evangelism, or gospel proclamation, is said to be sacred work. It therefore is more important. Work in the culture that aims for societal change based on biblical truths is secular, less important, and ultimately, a distraction.

The gospel is central to the biblical worldview, but the biblical worldview cannot be reduced to the gospel message alone. The biblical worldview provides answers to all the big questions including: questions of ultimate reality; human identity and purpose; and the source of, and solution to, evil in the world. Only in the context provided by this worldview does the gospel make any sense.

People need a comprehensive, overarching story of reality in order to make sense of their lives. If the church isn't out in the culture championing the true story—the biblical worldview— the only alternatives will be false and ultimately destructive worldviews. People cannot live without answers to the big questions of life and meaning. If ideological social justice is the only alternative, that is what people will embrace. The only way the church can effectively counter ideological social justice is with an equally comprehensive biblical worldview.

CHAPTER 8

DRIVING OUT A BAD WORLDVIEW BY OFFERING A BETTER ONE

I n a July 2018 article in *Quillette*, Barrett Wilson (not his real name) shared his story of his conversion into, and then out of, ideological social justice. It's a powerful reminder of how this toxic new religion effects the lives of real people. Wilson begins his story this way:

> I once had a well-paid job in what might be described as the social justice industry. . . . I was a self-righteous social justice crusader [who] would use my mid-sized Twitter and Facebook platforms to signal my wokeness on topics such as LGBT rights, rape culture, and racial injustice.

Wilson wasn't an academic. He likely knew very little about the neo-Marxist Antonio Gramsci or postmodern philosopher Michel Foucault. He likely couldn't explain the finer points of critical theory. Yet he had gravitated toward the ideology because it provided him with a story that made sense of his life, gave him a purpose, and membership in a community. He explains the attractiveness of ideological social justice this way:

> It was exhilarating. Every time I would call someone a racist or sexist, I would get a rush. That rush would then be affirmed and sustained by stars, hearts, and thumbs-up that constitute the nickels and dimes of social media validation. . . . When my callouts were met with approval and admiration, I was lavished with praise: "Thank you so much for speaking out!" "You're so brave!" "We need more men like you!"

Wilson had enlisted as a soldier in the social justice revolution. He and his comrades found their life's purpose in the fight against white supremacy, the patriarchy, transphobia, and toxic masculinity. He writes: "I went from minding my own business . . . to practically fainting when [people] used the wrong pronoun or expressed a right-of-center view." His days were spent patrolling the internet seeking out transgressors. Like all totalitarian systems past and present, Wilson reminds us that "Social justice is a surveillance culture, a snitch culture."

But like the earlier French and Russian Revolutionaries, Wilson discovered that the revolution can quickly turn on its own. That day had come for Wilson:

> I upset the wrong person, and within a short window of time, I was considered too toxic for my employer's taste. I was publicly shamed, mobbed, and reduced to a symbol of male privilege. I was cast out of my career and my professional community.

Wilson discovered that, ironically, in the world of ideological social justice, there is no justice for those accused of wrongdoing.

> There's no such thing as due process in this world. And once judgment has been rendered against you, the mob starts combing through your past, looking for similar transgressions that might have been missed.[1]

Others who have been "canceled" in this way have found the experience deeply traumatizing. Another proponent of ideological social justice, Karlyn Borysenko, described how she became "woke" to the true dangers of the religion. Many of her acquaintances "on Instagram were bullied and mobbed by hundreds of people for seemingly innocuous offenses. One man got mobbed so badly that he had a nervous breakdown and was admitted to the hospital on suicide watch. Many things were not right about the hatred, and witnessing the vitriol coming from those I had aligned myself with . . . was a massive wake-up call."[2]

Barrett and Karlyn represent millions of other young people who have been swept into the puritanical cult of ideological social justice. Many of them have never been to church or heard the gospel. They know little to nothing about the biblical worldview. For them, ideological social justice fills the hole in their soul for meaning, identity, and purpose. As Nathanael Blake said:

> The dogmas of intersectionality, socialism, gender theory, and other leftist notions of social justice are efforts to fill the void left by the decline of churches, communities, and families. But these secular doctrines are poor substitutes. . . . They bring rage and misery, not peace.[3]

The false religion of ideological social justice lures people by providing them with a source of identity, community, and purpose. But like any cult, once you are in, it is very hard to escape. According to Wilson: "The people giving me these stars, hearts and thumbs-up were engaging in their own cynical game: A fear of being targeted by the mob induces us to [virtue] signal publicly that we are part of it."[4]

My heart breaks when I read stories like this. Our calling is to boldly proclaim the truth that sets people free. How terrible and tragic that so many of our prominent evangelical leaders have abdicated their responsibility to be salt and light by promoting many of the central tenets of this dangerous, unbiblical worldview. Rather than proclaiming the truth that sets people free, they are pushing the very ideas that are destroying lives, fracturing relationships, and dividing our nations.

Even worse, by adopting the distorted, secularized definition of justice promoted by this ideology, they are disturbingly silent and disengaged when it comes to the greatest injustices and social evils of our day, like sex slavery, the persecution of Christians overseas, or abortion. Since 1973, more than 60 million innocent children have had their lives legally extinguished through abortion. This is a social evil on par with the greatest injustices in human history. We rightly despise the moral abomination of antebellum slavery, but legal abortion—including the trafficking of baby body parts for profit—is happening right now, *on our watch*. And yet, for those evangelicals who have drunken deeply from the fountain of ideological social justice, the fight against abortion, if engaged in at all, takes a back seat to issues like "demilitarizing" the police, lamenting systemic white racism, or deconstructing the criminal justice system.

People like Barrett and Karlyn don't need the church to validate their beliefs in ideological social justice. They need the church to offer a better story. A true story. A story that tells them that our true identity isn't found in our skin color, ethnic background, sex, or sexual orientation. Yes, we are shaped and influenced by our groups, but our groups don't define us. Our true identity is found in the fact that we are all unique and priceless human beings, made by God in His image, and loved deeply by Him. For God so loved Barrett and Karlyn—and you and me— "that he gave his one and only Son, that whoever believes in him shall not perish but have eternal life" (John 3:16).

They need to hear a story in which everyone bears God's image. Everyone has God-given endowments—a creative mind, a heart, hands, and a unique personality and gifts. They need to hear that rather than taking on the mantel of a "victim," God expects each of us to use these gifts and endowments to bless others, and to better our respective worlds. Everyone is capable, responsible, and accountable.

If your story tells you that your primary identity is "victim," your life will be marked by bitterness, resentment, grievance, and entitlement. If your story tells you your primary identity is privileged oppressor, your life will be marked by guilt and shame. However, if your story tells you that your identity is "sinner, yet loved by God and saved by grace," your life will be marked by gratitude and humility.

They need to hear a story in which power isn't ultimate, love is. In the false worldview of ideological social justice, truth and love don't exist. Everything boils down to a zero-sum contest of power between competing groups. But the Bible reveals that, for the sake of love, the most powerful being in the universe, the

Creator of all things, gave Himself up for us. God's only Son, in the immortal words of Philippians 2:5–8, "did not consider equality with God something to be used to his own advantage; rather, he made himself nothing by taking the very nature of a servant." He served us at the cost of His own life, given up on a cross, all because of love.

In the real world, many people, including many followers of Jesus Christ, have followed this example. Out of love for their neighbors, they have set aside their power and prerogatives, humbled themselves, and served others, even at great personal sacrifice.

Barrett and Karlyn need to hear a story in which the line between good and evil doesn't run between racial groups, or males and females, or any other group, class, or party. It runs right through every human heart. We all are sinners. We all, *equally*, are in need of grace and forgiveness. God extends His grace and forgiveness to all of us—equally—no matter our class, sex, ethnicity, or skin color. Because we are forgiven, He calls us to extend grace and forgiveness to one another as well. At the very heart of the biblical story is justice, but also mercy, grace, and forgiveness. Without these qualities woven into a culture, it will disintegrate.

Ultimately, they need to hear a story that defines what justice really is. In the counterfeit story they've absorbed, justice is the uprooting of traditional structures and systems, with the goal of redistributing power and money from so-called oppressor groups to victim groups in the pursuit of a utopian equality of outcome. This is a secular perversion of justice. In our story—the true story—justice is conformity to God's perfect moral law as found in the Ten Commandments and the royal law: "Love your neighbor as yourself" (James 2:8).

How will our neighbors who are in bondage to the false and destructive religion of ideological social justice know this powerful, life-changing, culture-transforming story unless God's people clearly, powerfully, and fearlessly communicate it in both word and deed?

To those many prominent evangelicals who are dabbling in, and ultimately supporting, this destructive counterfeit, either wittingly or unwittingly, I say this: The only thing you will accomplish is to further divide and weaken an already splintered church at a time when our broken, hurting nation desperately needs a strong, unified church fearlessly standing for truth.

"No thoughtful Christian . . . approves of true racism, injustice, or oppression when it exists," writes Scott Aniol, professor at Southwestern Baptist Theological Seminary. "But . . . by adopting these secular, leftist categories, which are rooted in ideologies explicitly intended to divide people, well-meaning Christians are making divides within Christianity and even broader society worse rather than better."[5]

Thankfully, many Christians are waking up to the dangers of ideological social justice. There are growing numbers of organized resistance movements. These efforts are vital. They are to be commended and supported. But as they speak out against this destructive worldview, it is important that they not merely oppose it, but instead uphold, defend, and proclaim the biblical worldview.

The fundamentalist movement of the past century opposed the social gospel. The social gospel was concerned with cultural reform, so the fundamentalists claimed that God wasn't interested in reforming society, but only in saving people out of this fallen world. The social gospel was concerned for the poor, so the fundamentalists claimed that concern for the poor was of secondary importance, and ultimately a distraction from the priority of evangelism.

The fundamentalist movement preserved the gospel, yet in its zeal to combat the social gospel, it also harmed the church by unintentionally abandoning the biblical worldview in favor of a quasi-biblical, Gnostic worldview that divided things that the Bible held together in equal priority. It prioritized the spiritual over the physical, evangelism over care for the poor, and full-time Christian ministry over work in the so-called "secular world."

Let's not repeat this mistake. Let's not simply be *anti*-ideological social justice. Let's be *pro*biblical worldview.

Here are some areas where opponents of ideological social justice need to be cautious:

HUMAN IDENTITY

Ideological social justice says that human beings are entirely socially determined, the product of their "identity groups" based on race, sex, and/or gender identity. In reaction, the temptation for opponents will be to swing to the opposite pole and view people merely as rugged individuals. This would be *anti*social justice but not *pro*biblical worldview. The biblical worldview sees humans *both* as unique individuals with agency, responsibility, and accountability, as well as members of communities that shape their identity, including families, churches, ethnic groups, and nationalities. The Bible affirms both aspects of our human nature and so must we.

CULTURAL TRANSFORMATION

Ideological social justice is revolutionary, calling the oppressed to rise up and overthrow their oppressors. That battle is carried out in the social, cultural, and political arenas. Tactically, the ends justify the means. Nothing is ruled out if it furthers the cause. For their brand of utopian, equality-of-outcome justice to be realized, it must be done in the here and now, by human power and cunning. There is no heaven, no afterlife, no future hope for an all-powerful, holy judge to put all wrongs to right.

In reaction, the temptation for opponents is to write-off Christian efforts to "engage the culture" or "transform the culture" as an unbiblical distraction from our spiritual purpose and mission—to save souls for heaven. This world is going to hell, so why bother trying to reform or change it for the better? Again, this attitude is *anti*social justice. It is not *pro*biblical worldview.

The biblical worldview sees this world as God's handiwork, and He loves His creation. His death on the cross isn't merely to save human souls out of the world, but to redeem all things broken through the fall. As it says in Colossians 1:15–20 (ESV, italics added):

> He [Jesus] is the image of the invisible God, the first-born of all creation. For by him all things were created, in heaven and on earth, visible and invisible, whether thrones or dominions or rulers or authorities—all things were created through him and for him. And he is before all things, and in him all things hold together. And he is the head of the body, the church. He is the beginning, the firstborn from the dead, that in

everything he might be preeminent. *For in him all the fullness of God was pleased to dwell, and through him to reconcile to himself all things, whether on earth or in heaven, making peace by the blood of his cross.*

God redeems us to participate with Him in reconciling all things to Himself. We are to be engaged in culture as ambassadors of Christ's kingdom. We are to work in the power of God's Spirit to bring truth, goodness, and beauty into every domain of human existence—into the arts, law, education, business, and government.

Of course the world is corrupt and falling apart. The gospel calls us to love and serve it nevertheless, with our eye toward that day when Christ will return and make all things new (Revelation 21:5). In the words of Francis Schaeffer, we should be working "on the basis of the finished work of Christ . . . [for] substantial healing now in every area where there are divisions [or brokenness] because of the Fall."[6] The biblical worldview sees evangelism and spiritual regeneration not as an end, but rather as a means to a larger end: the reconciliation of all things. Here's how New Testament theologian N. T. Wright puts it:

The great emphasis in the New Testament is that the gospel is not how to escape the world; the gospel is that the crucified and risen Jesus is the Lord of the world. And that his death and Resurrection transform the world, and that transformation can happen to you. You, in turn, can be part of the transforming work.[7]

As Christians committed to the biblical worldview, we too are passionate about working to transform this world—to see positive social and cultural change. We differ fundamentally on how this change happens. For the social justice revolutionary, the change is external to the human person. Unjust (unequal) social and cultural structures and systems must be replaced.

However, Christians believe that change must first be inward and spiritual before it can manifest itself externally in society and culture. The problems with the world are not "out there" in society; rather, they are "in here" in our fallen hearts and minds. All positive cultural change includes gospel proclamation and inward spiritual regeneration by the Holy Spirit. The antisocial justice mindset pits evangelism against social transformation. The biblical worldview, however, brings them together into a seamless whole: In the words of John Stott: "Evangelism is the major instrument of social change. For the gospel changes people, and changed people can change society."[8]

The temptation by opponents of ideological social justice to overreact by pitting evangelism and gospel proclamation against cultural engagement is a grievous error that must be avoided. This same overreaction by the fundamentalist movement against the social gospel did great damage to the witness of the church in the West for more than a hundred years. Evangelicals are only now beginning to recover our biblical understanding of mission. Let's learn from our own history and not fall back into this snare!

RACISM

Ideological social justice sees racism (and sexism, and homo/trans-phobia) as widespread, systemic, and pervasive. For its adherents, America, is so deeply stained by racism that the only hope is revolutionary change. In response, the temptation for the antisocial justice camp is to downplay racism or deny that it remains a significant problem in America. This is a mistake. While incredible progress has been made in overcoming racial discrimination, and while America today is one of the most ethnically diverse and tolerant societies in the world, racism remains a real problem—and not just for "whites."

Christians committed to a biblical worldview should reject the redefinition of racism popularized by critical race theory, namely, "prejudice plus power that only applies to white people." We should uphold and defend the true definition of racism— the belief that race is the primary determinant of human traits and capacities and that racial differences produce an inherent superiority of a particular race—and then work hard for racial reconciliation, while we expose and mortify our own racist thoughts and attitudes, and work to root racism out of our churches, institutions, and out of every corner of society.

STRUCTURAL, SYSTEMIC INJUSTICE

Because ideological social justice sees brokenness and injustice as rooted in social systems and structures as opposed to fallen human hearts, the temptation will be for opponents to deny or downplay the very idea of structural or systemic evil. This would be *anti*social justice, but not *pro*biblical worldview.

The biblical worldview provides a comprehensive view of the fall. It not only affects individuals, it disorders all of creation, including human-formed organizations, systems, and structures. God wants to redeem it all. We can agree with proponents of ideological social justice that structural or systemic evil exists. We need look no further than the pornography industry, which in the United States alone generates more than $2.5 billion in annual revenue and drives the evil of sex trafficking. Or we could look at Planned Parenthood and the abortion industry. These systemic evils should be torn down!

The fight against systemic social evil is not a distraction luring the church away from her central mission. No, this fight is fundamental to our calling. However, as Christians, we don't ignore what causes the fallen systems in the first place. If you want to reform evil structures and systems, you have to reform— or rather transform—fallen human hearts. In the words of pastor Grover Gunn: "Our primary means of transforming the world is through proclaiming the gospel. . . . We must today never question the effectiveness of the gospel message as the cutting edge of positive social change."[9] Many evangelical proponents of ideological social justice would be wise to remember this truth.

However, for a structure or system to be racist or sexist, certain criteria must apply. Ideological social justice advocates are known for throwing the terms "systemic" and "structural" around in a very generalized way, rarely getting specific about which policies or rules cause the whole system or structure to be racist, sexist, etc.

For something to be described as, for example, systemically racist, it is not merely enough to cite a disparity in outcome between whites and blacks or males and females. Take the example of student expulsions in Edina, Minnesota, public schools. It's true that more black students were expelled than white student relative to their overall population percentage. But that disparity doesn't prove institutional racism. Other factors need to be carefully examined before charging teachers or administrators with systemic racism. In this case, the behavior of the students themselves.

Advocates of ideological social justice rarely do this kind of careful analysis. Any disparity of outcome between races or sexes seems to be enough to level the very serious charge of systemic racism/sexism. This is a mistake. To my friends who wish to fight against systemic racism or sexism, I will be the first to stand shoulder-to-shoulder with you in your fight, but first, I need solid evidence that racism or sexism, and not some other reasonable cause, is at the root of the disparity. *Biblical justice demands this!* If you believe a system is racist or sexist, make your best case, put forward the facts and evidence. Be specific. If you do, you'll have many more Christians ready to stand with you in the fight.

WESTERN CIVILIZATION AND THE UNITED STATES OF AMERICA

The advocates of ideological social justice see Western civilization and the United States of America as irredeemably corrupted by systemic racism, sexism, greed, and almost every other kind of injustice. The temptation will be for opponents to swing to the opposite extreme and paint with their own very broad brush.

There are no perfect or even near-perfect civilizations or nations, America included. All are a mixed bag of good and evil, light and dark. Christians need to uphold the truth about our nation's history, both good and bad.

Americans are the beneficiaries of the sacrificial work done over many generations by committed Christians and non-Christians alike who have invested their lives in building a more perfect union. They sowed seeds of truth, goodness, and beauty into a political, economic, educational, and cultural order, which, while far from perfect, is tremendously blessed with freedom, justice, opportunity, and prosperity.

Today, many despise this inheritance. They choose only to be critical and to focus on the negative, ignoring all that is good (which is why it is called *critical* theory!). They want to throw it all away. This can be done, and tragically, is being done. However, I believe there are many more of us who are deeply grateful for our inheritance and, despite its flaws and imperfections, wish to preserve this inheritance and pass it along to future generations better than we received it.

Our attitude toward America, or Western civilization, shouldn't be marked by a negative, critical, and ungrateful spirit. Nor should it be marked by hubris or superiority. Instead, our attitude should be marked by humble gratitude. We are merely beneficiaries. We've inherited these blessings because of the labors of godly men and women who came before us and gave their all to build a nation on the truth of God's Word. Ultimately, our blessings come from God Himself.

TACTICS

Advocates of ideological social justice increasingly use power tactics to advance their narrative. Tactics like political correctness, bullying, shaming, threatening, deplatforming, silencing, and more.

Taken as a whole, these tactics are referred to as "cancel culture." Cancel culture doesn't believe in free speech, dialogue, or debate with ideological adversaries. It has no basis for civility or respect for ideological opponents. It believes in prevailing at all costs. The ends justify the means. In cancel culture, there is no forgiveness. No reconciliation. No grace. It is toxic—even demonic. It destroys the social fabric and rips apart relationships.

Nor are these power tactics new. They were standard practice in the French Revolution, and the communist revolutions in Russia, China, Cambodia, Cuba, and elsewhere. In fact, they are standard practice for Marxist revolutionaries everywhere.

HOW SHOULD CHRISTIAN OPPONENTS RESPOND?

There are two reactions that should be avoided. The first is to turn the tables in an attempt to use the same power tactics. But probably the bigger temptation is to be cowed into silence or submission. To keep your head down, pretend the war isn't raging around you, and try to go on with life as normal. This isn't sustainable. In a cultural revolution, they will eventually come for everyone.

The famous words of German theologian Martin Niemöller apply here:

> First they came for the socialists, and I did not speak out—
> Because I was not a socialist.
> Then they came for the trade unionists, and I did not speak out—
> Because I was not a trade unionist.
> Then they came for the Jews, and I did not speak out—
> Because I was not a Jew.
> Then they came for me—and there was no one left to speak for me.

Granted, evangelical advocates for ideological social justice typically don't engage in these power tactics in the same way their non-Christian compatriots do. Most will denounce them as well. But even among evangelicals who support ideological social justice, I've noticed a worrisome trend among them in avoiding dialogue and discussion with ideological opponents or even breaking off relationships.

Here are some thoughts on the right way to respond to ideological opponents:

- Always be gracious and civil, and not just in person, but also on social media.
- Give others the benefit of the doubt when it comes to their motives. Assume they genuinely want to pursue justice, fight for the oppressed, and stand against racism for biblical reasons.
- Be quick to listen, and slow to speak. Always try to learn and understand. Get the log out of your own eye first.
- Pray. Ask for God's help to engage in ways that honor and glorify Him. Pray that your opponents will turn from false beliefs and turn to the truth. Trust in God's supernatural power more than your own arguments or wisdom.
- Don't give up on engagement, discussion, and dialogue, even if your opponents do. You cannot control how they respond, but never be the first to break off relationship. Be quick to forgive. Quick to reconcile. Quick to affirm.
- Don't cow to pressure. Stand firm for the truth. Stand firm on biblical principles and biblical definitions. There is a mistaken idea that is now widespread in the evangelical community that "loving your neighbor" means affirming what they sincerely believe, even it is false and unbiblical.
- Loving your neighbor means sacrificially working for their good. Affirming their false beliefs may *seem* loving, but it isn't, because false beliefs are destructive. They never lead to freedom or flourishing.

- Don't fear, but trust in God's sovereignty and power. Our opponents *are* powerful. They have massive amounts of cultural support in the media, the entertainment business, government agencies, various businesses, and on social media. They have seemingly unlimited amounts of money backing their cause.

But never forget that God loves using the weak things of the world to show His surpassing power and glory. Remember David and Goliath? Gideon and the Midianites? The uneducated fisherman Peter before the Sanhedrin? That same God is alive and well today. He isn't surprised by what is happening. If He is for us, who can be against us (Romans 8:31)?

How does God respond to worldly powers and authorities who plot and scheme against Him and His people? *He laughs.*

Why do the nations conspire and the peoples plot in vain?

The kings of the earth rise up and the rulers band together against the LORD and against his anointed, saying: "Let us break their chains and throw off their shackles."

The One enthroned in heaven laughs; the Lord scoffs at them. He rebukes them in his anger, and terrifies them in his wrath, saying, "I have installed my king on Zion, my holy mountain." (Psalm 2:1–6)

Pay close attention to the words of Jesus:

"Do not be afraid of those who kill the body [or remove your Facebook account or take away your job or destroy your reputation] but cannot kill the soul.

Rather, be afraid of the One who can destroy both soul and body in hell." (Matthew 10:28)

"Blessed are you when people insult you, persecute you and falsely say all kinds of evil against you because of me. Rejoice and be glad, because great is your reward in heaven; for in the same way they persecuted the prophets who were before you." (Matthew 5:11–12)

Love those who oppose you and pray for them (Matthew 5:44). Christ's kingdom advances as truth is proclaimed and demonstrated in love (Ephesians 4:15). "Do not be overcome by evil, but overcome evil with good" (Romans 12:21).

LET'S MOVE BEYOND CRITICIZING CULTURE, TO CREATING CULTURE.

The fact that evangelicalism no longer has a strong theology of cultural engagement is perhaps the main reason we are in our present dilemma. The key institutions shaping our culture— education, the arts, film, literature and entertainment, law, and business—are almost entirely controlled by those operating from the presuppositions of ideological social justice.

This didn't happen by accident. The champions of this worldview have a missionary "theology," and a zeal that was common among Christians of earlier generations. Our forebears in the faith founded world-class universities all across the globe, including Yale, Harvard, and Princeton. They did this in order to influence the broader culture in ways that honored our King and blessed our neighbors. But then we lost our way. We almost entirely stopped doing this kind of work. Our theology of mission was reduced to numbers: How many souls saved?

How many churches planted? How many people in the church on Sunday? God didn't care about the culture. It was fallen and worldly, destined for destruction.

The champions of ideological social justice, however, didn't lose their vision for impacting the culture—you might even say "discipling" the nation. Their strategy was to influence the main drivers of culture, and they have been incredibly intentional and patient in carrying out their "long march through the institutions." Give them credit. They are now reaping the reward of years of diligent perseverance.

They were very intentional, for example, in reforming our systems of education along the lines if ideological social justice, paying particular attention to the schools of education, curriculum, and teacher training, which today are almost entirely governed by the presuppositions of ideological social justice. The idea that education is "unbiased" or "neutral" is a myth. It will always be built upon a particular view of truth, morality, human nature, history, and much more. These views will always be informed by a deeper set of presuppositions, or worldviews. If not the biblical worldview, then another one.

My friend and mentor Darrow Miller is fond of saying, "If the church fails to disciple the nation, the nation will disciple the church." Someone is always actively impacting culture. If it isn't the followers of Jesus, it will be, by default, those who adhere to another worldview. If we don't like the worldview that is shaping our culture, we only have ourselves to blame.

The hour is late, but I believe there is still time, We, the Bible-believing church, must quickly re-learn from our forebears what genuine Christian mission should be. We need to recover that older theology that seamlessly links the gospel, evangelism, and discipleship with faithfully living out the implications of the biblical worldview in every area of life and every sphere of society. After all, Jesus isn't merely King over some limited, spiritual area. He is King of heaven and earth! We need to remember this, and act like it. We need to get back into the business of institutional formation and culture creation, particularly in the areas of education, the arts, media, law, and business. We need to be just as strategic, patient, and intentional as our ideological opponents have been. Our motive must be driven by obedience to Christ, who raised up a people for Himself to bless all the nations, and to love our neighbors as ourselves. Only biblical truth and love leads to flourishing and freedom—and not just for the church, but for Christians and non-Christians alike.

Ideological social justice is dangerous because it is false. It is building a culture of hatred, division, a false sense of moral superiority, and a false understanding of justice. A culture where truth is replaced by power, and gratitude by ingratitude. A culture where everyone seeks out opportunities to be aggrieved and put on the mantle of the victim. A culture where people don't take responsibility for their lives, but instead blame all their problems on others. A culture of sexual libertinism and personal autonomy, where "sexual desire is the center of human identity and dignity." A culture where your identity is wholly defined by your tribe, and your tribe is always in conflict with other tribes in a zero-sum competition for power.

In this culture, there is no "love your neighbors," much less "love your enemies." There is no grace. No forgiveness. No humility. No introspection that gets "the log out of your own eye" before you correct your opponent.

Do you want to live in this kind of culture, much less participate in building it? Not me. I want to live in a culture where truth, justice, and love are the highest goods. A culture where God is honored as King, and all people, regardless of their race, sex, or class are respected and loved as His beloved children. A culture where people are judged by "the content of their character, not the color of their skin." A culture in which justice is based on God's unchanging moral law, and those accused of injustice are treated with fairness and impartiality. A culture that upholds due process and the rule of law. A country that sees all people as fallen sinners, yet objects of God's love, mercy, and forgiveness. A culture marked by grace, mercy, tolerance, and forgiveness. A culture where reconciliation and redemption are possible. A culture marked by humble gratitude.

This culture still exists in America today.

In June 2015 the world saw the worst that human beings can do to one another. One evening, white supremacist Dylann Roof, aged twenty-one, walked into the Emanuel African Methodist Episcopal Church in Charleston, South Carolina, and gunned down nine African American men and women who were participating in a Bible study. The authorities quickly caught up with Roof, arresting and eventually convicting him of murder.

At Roof's sentencing hearing, many of the surviving family members stood up in court, not merely to list their justified grievances, but to forgive him. Nadine Collier, the daughter of Ethel Lance, one of the victims, told Roof, "I will never be able to hold her again, but I forgive you and have mercy on your soul. You hurt me. You hurt a lot of people, but God forgives you, and I forgive you."

Anthony Thompson told his wife's killer, "I forgive you, and my family forgives you. But we would like you to take this opportunity to repent. Change your ways."[10]

Corrie ten Boom tells a similar story. A Dutch Christian, Ten Boom, along with her family members, helped many Jews to escape Nazi genocide. Eventually, however, the Gestapo discovered what they were doing and sent Corrie and several family members to prison. While her sister Betsie and her father, Casper, died in German custody, Corrie survived. Here she tells the gripping account of later confronting a Nazi officer in the prison where Betsie died.

It was in a church in Munich that I saw him, a balding heavyset man in a gray overcoat, a brown felt hat clutched between his hands. People were filing out of the basement room where I had just spoken, moving along the rows of wooden chairs to the door at the rear.

It was 1947 and I had come from Holland to defeated Germany with the message that God forgives. . . .

And that's when I saw him, working his way forward against the others. One moment I saw the overcoat and the brown hat; the next, a blue uniform and a visored cap with its skull and crossbones.

It came back with a rush: the huge room with its harsh overhead lights, the pathetic pile of dresses and shoes in the center of the floor, the shame of walking naked past this man. I could see my sister's frail form ahead of me, ribs sharp beneath the parchment skin. Betsie, how thin you were!

Betsie and I had been arrested for concealing Jews in our home during the Nazi occupation of Holland; this man had been a guard at Ravensbrück concentration camp where we were sent.

Now he was in front of me, hand thrust out: "A fine message, *fräulein*! How good it is to know that, as you say, all our sins are at the bottom of the sea!"

And I, who had spoken so glibly of forgiveness, fumbled in my pocketbook rather than take that hand. He would not remember me, of course—how could he remember one prisoner among those thousands of women?

But I remembered him and the leather crop swinging from his belt. It was the first time since my release that I had been face to face with one of my captors and my blood seemed to freeze.

"You mentioned Ravensbrück in your talk," he was saying. "I was a guard in there." No, he did not remember me.

"But since that time," he went on, "I have become a Christian. I know that God has forgiven me for the cruel things I did there, but I would like to hear it from your lips as well. *Fräulein*"—again the hand came out—"will you forgive me?"

And I stood there—I whose sins had every day to be forgiven—and could not. Betsie had died in that place—could he erase her slow terrible death simply for the asking?

It could not have been many seconds that he stood there, hand held out, but to me it seemed hours as I wrestled with the most difficult thing I had ever had to do. . . .

And still I stood there with the coldness clutching my heart. But forgiveness is not an emotion—I knew that too. Forgiveness is an act of the will, and the will can function regardless of the temperature of the heart.

"Jesus, help me!" I prayed silently. "I can lift my hand. I can do that much. You supply the feeling."

And so woodenly, mechanically, I thrust my hand into the one stretched out to me. And as I did, an incredible thing took place. The current started in my shoulder, raced down my arm, sprang into our joined hands. And then this healing warmth seemed to flood my whole being, bringing tears to my eyes.

"I forgive you, brother!" I cried. "With all my heart!"[11]

The kind of supernatural love and forgiveness demonstrated by Corrie Ten Boom, Anthony Thompson, and others at Emanuel African Methodist Episcopal Church in South Carolina is a true revolution. The revolution of Jesus Christ. They amaze us because they possessed a power to forgive their enemies. That power came, in part, from a recognition that they too are sinners forgiven by God and objects of His amazing, extraordinary grace.

Rather than seeking vengeance, they entrusted ultimate judgment into God's hands. So should we, knowing that He has promised to set all things right.

These kinds of stories are possible only in cultures that have been deeply shaped by the Transforming Story—the truth of the biblical worldview. It is powerful. It is deeply beautiful. It is good. It is true.

How do we Christians respond to ideological social justice? Do we merely react against it, or do we offer a better alternative? Nancy Pearcey is exactly right:

> The best way to drive out a bad worldview is by offering a good one, and Christians need to move beyond criticizing culture to creating culture. That is the task God originally created humans to do, and in the process of sanctification we are meant to recover that task. . . . In every calling we are culture-creators, offering up our work as service to God.[12]

This is a dangerous moment for evangelicals in the West. Our confusion over justice needs to be replaced by careful discernment. If we continue to allow the yeast of social justice to contaminate our theology at a time when the culture desperately needs to see true, biblical justice advocated and lived out, the losses will be incalculable, both in time and in eternity. As well, if we throw out the biblical justice baby with the social justice bathwater, those who care for the oppressed will rightly call us hypocrites. Not for nothing does the Lord say to hypocrites, "The name of God is blasphemed among the Gentiles because of you" (Romans 2:24 ESV).

So let's fight for justice in this world. Let's fight for the victims of injustice. Let's oppose sex trafficking. Female infanticide. The unborn at risk in their mothers' wombs. Those persecuted for their beliefs, Christian and non-Christian. Let's speak up for those facing execution unjustly. These fellow image-bearers are not facing microaggressions. They are facing macroaggressions, including torture and violent death.

Standing up against injustice in a fallen world, of course, requires moral courage. The perpetrators of injustice often hold powerful positions. The Old Testament prophets often spoke against the powerful, and many paid a heavy price. As the book of Hebrews marvels, "[They] suffered mocking and flogging, and even chains and imprisonment. They were stoned, they were sawn in two, they were killed with the sword. They went about in skins of sheep and goats, destitute, afflicted, mistreated—of whom the world was not worthy—wandering about in deserts and mountains, and in dens and caves of the earth" (Hebrews 11:36–38 ESV).

To challenge the powers that be is to open yourself up to suffering and loss. The temptation to remain silent is great, but we must reject that temptation. The Westminster Larger Catechism warns against "undue silence in a just cause, and holding our peace when iniquity call[s] for either a reproof from ourselves, or complaint to others."

As Christians, however, we can be confident that our lives are secure in Jesus Christ, and nothing, including death itself, can separate us from His love (Romans 8:31–38). Empowered by the Holy Spirit, we are to follow in the footsteps of our Savior and pursue justice and mercy. As the Lord said, "The Spirit of the Lord is upon me, because he has anointed me to proclaim good news to the poor. He has sent me to proclaim liberty to the captives and recovering of sight to the blind, to set at liberty those who are oppressed" (Luke 4:18).

Extending God's kingdom rule is a holy task, and sometimes a lonely one, but we are never really alone. As Greg Koukl reminds us, "Those of us who trust Him are not alone in the struggles against evil and injustice. Even though we take casualties, He is with us, always, in everything. That is His promise. 'In this world you will have tribulation, Jesus told us. But take courage. I have overcome the world.'"[13]

We can trust the God who brought justice and mercy together perfectly at the cross to be with us as we promote justice for His glory. Since justice ultimately is God's work, God's representatives must do it in God's way—not by overcoming evil with evil but, following the example of Corrie ten Boom and the members of Emanuel African Methodist Episcopal Church, by overcoming evil with good.

> *Now all has been heard;*
> *here is the conclusion of the matter:*
> *Fear God and keep his commandments,*
> *for this is the duty of all mankind.*
> *For God will bring every deed into judgment,*
> *including every hidden thing,*
> *whether it is good or evil.*
> —Ecclesiastes 12:13

ACKNOWLEDGMENTS

To my beloved wife, Kimberly, and our wonderful children Kaila, Jenna, Luke, Isaac, and Annelise, who spent many hours listening to me ramble on about the contents of this book, and provided so much support, feedback, and inspiration. Thank you from the bottom of my heart.

To my dear friends, mentors, and co-workers at the Disciple Nations Alliance: Darrow Miller, Bob Moffitt, Dwight Vogt, Jessie Christensen, Shawn Carson, Jeff Wright, Gary Brumbelow, John Bottimore, Jon Taylor, Eric Dalrymple, Blake Williams, Heather Hicks, Gary Paisley, and Bob Evans. Without your help, support, ideas, discussions, and critiques, this book would have never been completed. Your partnership in ministry means the world to me. Thank you.

To many new and old friends and colleagues, including Carolyn Beckett, Kelly Kullberg, Wayne Grudem, Marvin Olasky, Clay Howerton, Elizabeth Youmans, and George Tingom, who offered special help, support, and encouragement at just the right time. You are a gift from God to me. Thank you.

I would also like to thank Neil Shenvi, Os Guinness, and Tom Ascol. Your teaching has done so much to mentor me on my own journey to understand critical social theory and the threat it poses to the church. While many others have helped, you in particular have inspired me with your keen intellect, grace, courage, and passion for God and His people. As you know, this can be a difficult and discouraging journey, but following your lead has been a source of great encouragement to me.

To the very talented and professional wordsmiths and editors, Stan Guthrie and Elizabeth Banks, thank you for your outstanding work. And to Tim Beals, publisher of Credo House Publishing, your eagerness and enthusiasm for this project, after many rejections, was a true answer to prayer. It means so much to me. Thank you.

A special thanks to Bob Osburn, Executive Director of the Wilberforce Academy, who was one of the first to believe in the importance of this book. You believed that God was calling me to write it, even when I didn't. Without your gentle and persistent encouragement to keep going, this book would never have been written. I'm so blessed to count you as a friend and co-worker in ministry. Thank you from the bottom of my heart.

To Jesus, the lover of my soul, my King and my redeemer. Thank you, forever, thank you.

Soli Deo Gloria.

ENDNOTES

Introduction

1   John Stonestreet, "What Is Freedom? Defining Liberty Is Crucial to Keeping It," CNSNews.com, October 4, 2018, https://www.cnsnews.com/commentary/john-stonestreet/what-freedom-defining-liberty-crucial-keeping-it.

2   Dallas Willard, *The Divine Conspiracy: Rediscovering Our Hidden Life in God* (San Francisco: HarperOne, 2009).

3   Robert Lewis Wilken, "The Church as Culture," First Things, April 2004, https://www.firstthings.com/article/2004/04/the-church-as-culture.

4   Andrew Sullivan, "We All Live on Campus Now," New York Intelligencer, February 9, 2018, https://nymag.com/intelligencer/2018/02/we-all-live-on-campus-now.html.

5   My colleague Darrow Miller, along with Gary Brumbelow and myself, wrote a book on this subject titled *Rethinking Social Justice: Restoring Biblical Compassion* (Seattle, WA: YWAM, 2015).

Chapter 1

1   Matthew Bunson, "The State of the Union: 'Let Us Build a Culture That Cherishes Innocent Life,'" *National Catholic Register*, February 6, 2019, http://www.ncregister.com/blog/mbunson/the-state-of-the-union-let-us-build-a-culture-that-cherishes-innocent-life.

2   ABC News Politics Twitter feed, February 5, 2019, https://twitter. com/ABCPolitics/status/1092997836252209157.

3   "Reproductive Justice," SisterSong, https://www.sistersong.net/ reproductive-justice.

4   Allyson Hunter, "Study Shows the Leading Cause of Death Is Abortion," Texas Right to Life, August 3, 2018, https://www. texasrighttolife.com/study-shows-the-leading-cause-of-death- is-abortion/.

5   Jason L. Riley, "Let's Talk about the Black Abortion Rate," *The Wall Street Journal*, July 10, 2018, https://www.wsj.com/articles/ lets-talk-about-the-black-abortion-rate-1531263697.

6   Ryan Scott Bomberger, "The Democrat Party: Not Enough African- Americans Aborted," The Radiance Foundation, February 1, 2019, http://www.theradiancefoundation.org/blackhistorymonth/.

7   Ross Douthat, "The Tom Cotton Op-Ed and the Cultural Revolution," *New York Times*, June 12, 2020, https://www.nytimes. com/2020/06/12/opinion/nyt-tom-cotton-oped-liberalism.html.

8   Graham Hillard, "The Social-Justice Movement's Unjust Crusade," *National Review*, March 7, 2019, https://www.nationalreview. com/magazine/2019/03/25/the-social-justice-movements- unjust-crusade/.

9   Nancy Pearcey, "Midterms Bring Out the Marxists," *American Thinker*, November 5, 2018, https://www.americanthinker.com/ articles/2018/11/midterms_bring_out_the_marxists.html.

10   Ed Stetzer, "InterVarsity, #BlackLivesMatter, Criticism, and Three Suggestions for the Future," *Christianity Today*, January 4, 2016, https://www.christianitytoday.com/edstetzer/2016/january/ intervarsity-race-criticism-and-future.html.

11   Tobin Grant, "InterVarsity Backs #BlackLivesMatters [sic] at Urbana 15," Religion News Service, December 29, 2015, https://religionnews.com/2015/12/29/intervarsity-backs- blacklivesmatters-at-urbana-15/.

12 Black Lives Matter, https://blacklivesmatter.com/our-co-founders/.

13 Ibid.

14 Black Lives Matter, https://blacklivesmatter.com/what-we-believe/.

15 See Lisa Sharon Harper, "Open Letter to the Leadership of #Urbana15 and InterVarsity Christian Fellowship," *Sojourners*, January 5, 2016, https://sojo.net/articles/open-letter-leadership-urbana15-and-intervarsity-christian-fellowship.

Chapter 2

1 http://webstersdictionary1828.com/.

2 Webster's 1828 Dictionary: "Justice: The virtue which consists in giving to everyone what is his due; practical conformity to the laws and to principles of rectitude in the dealings of men with each other; honesty; integrity in commerce or mutual intercourse. Justice is distributive or commutative. Distributive justice belongs to magistrates or rulers, and consists in distributing to every man that right or equity which the laws and the principles of equity require; or in deciding controversies according to the laws and to principles of equity. Commutative justice consists in fair dealing in trade and mutual intercourse between man and man."

3 http://web.cn.edu/kwheeler/documents/letter_birmingham_jail.pdf.

4 Gregory Koukl, *The Story of Reality* (Grand Rapids: Zondervan Publishing House, 2017), 76.

5 As discussed in R. C. Sproul's "Which Laws Apply?" Ligonier Ministries, https://www.ligonier.org/learn/articles/which-laws-apply/.

6 Daniel Janosik, "Is Allah of Islam the Same as Yahweh of Christianity?" Columbia International University, http://www.ciu.edu/content/allah-islam-same-yahweh-christianity.

7 Ken Wytsma, *Pursuing Justice* (Nashville: Thomas Nelson, 2013), 89.

8 C. S. Lewis, *Mere Christianity* (New York: Macmillan, 1952), 21.

9   "Natural Law," New Advent, http://www.newadvent.org/cathen/09076a.htm.

10   As quoted in Wytsma, 95.

11   Kevin DeYoung, "Is Social Justice a Gospel Issue?" The Gospel Coalition, September 11, 2018, https://www.thegospelcoalition.org/blogs/kevin-deyoung/social-justice-gospel-issue/.

12   Tim Keller, "What Is Biblical Justice?" *Relevant*, August 23, 2012, https://relevantmagazine.com/god/practical-faith/what-biblical-justice.

13   http://www.ushistory.org/declaration/document/.

14   See, for example, Deuteronomy 6:4–5; Mark 12:30–31.

15   Koukl, 97.

16   Ravi Zacharias, *Jesus Among Other Gods and Deliver Us from Evil* (The Two in One Volume), (Nashville: Thomas Nelson, 2009), 84.

17   "Anecdotes and Illustrations—Dwight L. Moody," Precept Austin, https://www.preceptaustin.org/anecdotes_and_illustrations-moody.

18   Exodus 20; Matthew 5–7, respectively.

19   Koukl, 79.

20   Koukl, 78.

21   Paraphrased from Koukl, 154.

Chapter 3

1   Quoted in Murray Campbell, "Rachael Denhollander and Her Extraordinary Speech," The Gospel Coalition, January 25, 2018, https://au.thegospelcoalition.org/article/rachael-denhollander-extraordinary-speech/. Other Denhollander quotes in the following text are also from this article.

2   John Piper, "Christ Overcame Evil with Good—Do the Same," Desiring God, March 20, 2005, https://www.desiringgod.org/messages/christ-overcame-evil-with-good-do-the-same.

3   See "It Is the Ligament," LawMuseum, http://www.duhaime.org/LawMuseum/LawArticle-558/It-Is-The-Ligament.aspx.

4   C. S. Lewis, *The Weight of Glory* (San Francisco: HarperOne, 2001), 45–46.

5   Sarah Irving-Stonebraker, "How Oxford and Peter Singer Drove Me from Atheism to Jesus," Solas, May 6, 2019, https://www. solas-cpc.org/how-oxford-and-peter-singer-drove-me-from-atheism-to-jesus/?fbclid=IwAR1TaXvR4LLGyMJlXhGiYNPMG Jk_KasEYaVY4by7H-4lZ9APM_kmqfiTsjo.

6   Brian Flood, "*New York Times* stands by new tech writer Sarah Jeong after racist tweets surface," Fox News, August 2, 2018, https:// www.foxnews.com/entertainment/new-york-times-stands-by-new-tech-writer-sarah-jeong-after-racist-tweets-surface.

7   https://www.transparency.org/research/cpi/overview.

8   For more information on this topic, see "The Elements of Due Process," Legal Information Institute, https://www.law. cornell.edu/constitution-conan/amendment-14/section-1/the-elements-of-due-process.

Chapter 4

1   Noah Rothman quoted in Graham Hillard, "The Social-Justice Movement's Unjust Crusade," *National Review*, March 25, 2019, https://www.nationalreview.com/magazine/2019/03/25/the-social-justice-movements-unjust-crusade/.

2   I'm indebted to Everett Piper, former president of Oklahoma Wesleyan University for these insights.

3   *Planned Parenthood v. Casey*, United States Supreme Court, 505 US 833; 112 S.Ct. 2791; 120 L.Ed. 2d. 674 (1992), https://web.utk. edu/~scheb/decisions/Casey.htm.

4   For an in-depth treatment of this important history, I recommend Nancy Pearcey's *Finding Truth: 5 Principles for Unmasking Atheism, Secularism, and Other God Substitutes* (Colorado Springs: David C. Cook, 2015). See also Peggy Kamuf, "When Derrida Discovered Marx," Salon, April 28, 2013, https://www.salon.com/2013/04/28/grappling_with_specters_of_marx_partner/.

5   For more on this topic, see Nicki Lisa Cole, PhD, "The Frankfurt School of Critical Theory: An Overview of People and Theory," ThoughtCo., January 11, 2019, https://www.thoughtco.com/frankfurt-school-3026079.

6   Pearcey, "Midterms Bring Out the Marxists."

7   A very similar diagram can be found in Sensoy and DiAngelo's *Is Everyone Really Equal? An Introduction to Key Concepts in Social Justice Education*, Figure 5.1, or Adams' *Teaching for Diversity and Social Justice* Fig. 3.2 or Appendix C.

8   See Paul Austin Murphy, "Antonio Gramsci: Take Over the Institutions!" *American Thinker*, April 26, 2014, https://www.americanthinker.com/articles/2014/04/antonio_gramsci_take_over_the_institutions.html.

9   Shulamith Firestone, "The Dialectic of Sex" (chapter 1 reprinted from the book of the same name; London, UK: The Women's Press, 1979), https://www.marxists.org/subject/women/authors/firestone-shulamith/dialectic-sex.htm, italics in original.

10   Quoted in Al Mohler, "Why Religion, If Not Based in Truth, Is Grounded in Nothing More Than Moral Aspirations," *The Briefing*, December 19, 2018, https://albertmohler.com/2018/12/19/briefing-12-19-18/.

11   Nancy Pearcey, *Total Truth: Liberating Christianity from Its Cultural Captivity* (Wheaton, IL: Crossway Books, 2004), 11.

12   Dallas Willard, *Knowing Christ Today* (New York: HarperCollins, 2009).

13   John Stott, *Issues Facing Christians Today*, Fourth Edition (Grand Rapids: Zondervan, 2006).

14   Neil Shenvi, "Social Justice, Critical Theory, and Christianity: Are They Compatible?—Part 3," https://shenviapologetics.com/social-justice-critical-theory-and-christianity-are-they-compatible-part-3-2/.

Chapter 5

1   James A. Lindsay and Mike Nayna, "Postmodern Religion and the Faith of Social Justice," *Areo*, December 18, 2018, https://areomagazine.com/2018/12/18/postmodern-religion-and-the-faith-of-social-justice/.

2   Francis A. Schaeffer, *A Christian Manifesto* (Wheaton, IL: Crossway Books, 1981), 18.

3   Nancy Pearcey, *Finding Truth* (Colorado Springs: David C. Cook, 2015), 118.

4   Jordan Peterson, "On Claiming Belief in God: Commentary and Discussion with Dennis Prager," *The Jordan B. Peterson Podcast*, July 7, 2019, https://www.jordanbpeterson.com/podcast/s2-e16-on-claiming-belief-in-god-commentary-discussion-with-dennis-prager/.

5   See Elianna Johnson, "The Road to Yale's Free-Speech Crisis," *National Review*, July 5, 2016, https://www.nationalreview.com/2016/07/yale-free-speech/.

6   Ta-Nehisi Coates, "The First White President," *The Atlantic*, October 2017, https://www.theatlantic.com/magazine/archive/2017/10/the-first-white-president-ta-nehisi-coates/537909/.

7   Carlos Lozada, "The Radical Chic of Ta-Nehisi Coates," *The Washington Post*, July 16, 2015, https://www.washingtonpost.com/news/book-party/wp/2015/07/16/the-radical-chic-of-ta-nehisi-coates/.

8   Bradford Richardson, "Gay Megadonor on Going After Christians," *Washington Times*, July 19, 2017, https://www.washingtontimes.com/news/2017/jul/19/gay-megadonor-going-after-christians-punish-wicked/.

9   Philippe Leonard Fradet, "7 Reasons Why Patriarchy Is Bad (And Feminism Is Good) For Men," *Everyday Feminism Magazine*, November 14, 2016, https://everydayfeminism.com/2016/11/patriarchy-bad-for-men/.

10   As quoted in Stephen Miller, "Intersectionality for Dummies," *The Weekly Standard*, January 19, 2018, https://www.weeklystandard.com/stephen-miller/intersectionality-for-dummies.

11   Stella Morabito, "*The New York Times* Has Embraced the Bigotry of Identity Politics," *The Federalist*, August 16, 2018, https://thefederalist.com/2018/08/06/the-new-york-times-embraces-bigoted-identity-politics-in-jeong-hire/.

12   Michiko Kakutani, "Review: In 'Between the World and Me,' Ta-Nehisi Coates Delivers a Searing Dispatch to His Son," *The New York Times*, July 9, 2015, https://www.nytimes.com/2015/07/10/books/review-in-between-the-world-and-me-ta-nehisi-coates-delivers-a-desperate-dispatch-to-his-son.html.

13   Justin Taylor, "Aleksandr Solzhenitsyn: 'Bless You, Prison!'" *The Gospel Coalition*, October 14, 2011, https://www.thegospelcoalition.org/blogs/justin-taylor/aleksandr-solzhenitsyn-bless-you-prison/.

14   Nikki Schwab, "Anne Hathaway Denounces White Privilege in Award Speech," *New York Post*, September 16, 2018, https://nypost.com/2018/09/16/anne-hathaway-denounces-white-privilege-in-award-speech/.

15   Rod Dreher, "Beating the Cultural Revolution," *The American Conservative*, March 8, 2019, https://www.theamericanconservative.com/dreher/beating-the-cultural-revolution/.

16   Peggy Noonan, "Get Ready for the Struggle Session," *The Wall Street Journal*, March 7, 2019, https://www.wsj.com/articles/get-ready-for-the-struggle-session-11552003346.

17   Dallas Willard, *Renovation of the Heart: Putting On the Character of Christ* (Colorado Springs: NavPress, 2012), 15.

18   Grover Gunn, "Making Waves," *Tabletalk* from Ligonier Ministries and R. C. Sproul, January 2001, 13.

19   Stott, *Issues Facing Christians Today*.

20   From C. S. Lewis's postscript to *The Screwtape Letters*, quoted in "Illustrated Screwtape," http://www.cslewis.com/illustrated-screwtape/.

21 Steve Inskeep, "Hidden Brain: America's Changing Attitudes toward Gay People," *Morning Edition*, National Public Radio, April 17, 2019, https://www.npr.org/2019/04/17/714212984/hidden-brain-americas-changing-attitudes-toward-gay-people.

22 "Homosexuality, gender and religion," Pew Research Center, October 5, 2017, https://www.people-press.org/2017/10/05/5-homosexuality-gender-and-religion/.

23 Katy Steinmetz, "See Obama's 20-Year Evolution on LGBT Rights," *Time*, April 10, 2015, http://time.com/3816952/obama-gay-lesbian-transgender-lgbt-rights/.

24 Jayme Metzgar, "Hate Hoaxes Are What Happen When Your Religion Is Identity Politics," *The Federalist*, February 20, 2019, https://thefederalist.com/2019/02/20/hate-hoaxes-happen-religion-identity-politics/.

25 Rod Dreher, "The Race War the Left Wants," *The American Conservative*, May 24, 2019, https://www.theamericanconservative.com/dreher/the-race-war-the-left-wants/.

26 Ta-Nehisi Coates, *We Were Eight Years in Power: An American Tragedy*, quoted at https://www.goodreads.com/quotes/8853853-perhaps-after-a-serious-discussion-and-debate---the-kind.

27 Metzgar, "Hate Hoaxes."

28 As quoted in Scott Allen, "Core Doctrines of the New Religion: Group Identity and Cultural Relativism," Darrow Miller and Friends, May 22, 2017, http://darrowmillerandfriends.com/2017/05/22/core-doctrines-new-religion/.

29 Andrew Freundlich, "Feminist Standpoint Epistemology and Objectivity," *The Compass Rose: Explorations in Thought*, May 3, 2016, https://wordpress.viu.ca/compassrose/feminist-standpoint-epistemology-and-objectivity/.

30 Robert Tracinski, "No, GOP's Obamacare Update Doesn't Make Rape a Pre-Existing Condition," The Federalist, May 8, 2017, https://thefederalist.com/2017/05/08/no-gops-obamacare-update-doesnt-make-rape-pre-existing-condition/.

31   As quoted in Albert Mohler, "Religious Freedom and Discrimination: Why the Debate Continues," The Gospel Coalition, June 28, 2017, https://www.thegospelcoalition.org/reviews/debating-religious-liberty-and-discrimination/.

32   Pearcey, *Finding Truth*, 120.

33   James A. Lindsay and Mike Nayna, "Postmodern Religion and the Faith of Social Justice," *Areo*, December 18, 2018, https://areomagazine.com/2018/12/18/postmodern-religion-and-the-faith-of-social-justice/comment-page-1/.

34   Sinan Aral, "How Lies Spread Online," *The New York Times*, March 8, 2018, https://www.nytimes.com/2018/03/08/opinion/sunday/truth-lies-spread-online.html.

35   Charles J. Chaput, "The Splendor of Truth in 2017," *First Things*, October 2017, https://www.firstthings.com/article/2017/10/the-splendor-of-truth-in-2017.

36   Jonathan Haidt, "Coddle U vs. Strengthen U: What a Great University Should Be," *The Righteous Mind*, October 6, 2017, https://righteousmind.com/author/jonathan-haidt-2/page/3/.

37   Conor Friedersdorf, "The Rise of Victimhood Culture," *The Atlantic*, September 11, 2015, https://www.theatlantic.com/politics/archive/2015/09/the-rise-of-victimhood-culture/404794/.

38   An excellent summary of *critical theory* is available from *The Stanford Encyclopedia of Philosophy*, https://plato.stanford.edu/entries/critical-theory/.

39   Lindsay and Nayna, https://areomagazine.com/2018/12/18/postmodern-religion-and-the-faith-of-social-justice/.

40   John Stonestreet, president of BreakPoint and The Colson Center, is my source for this statement.

Chapter 6

1   Quoted at "Lewis on Democracy," cslewis.com, http://www.
     cslewis.com/lewis-on-democracy/.

2   Timothy B. Lee, "Google Fired James Damore for a Controversial
     Gender Memo—Now He's Suing," *Ars Technica*, January 9, 2018,
     https://arstechnica.com/tech-policy/2018/01/lawsuit-goes-after-
     alleged-anti-conservative-bias-at-google/.

3   Katherine Kersten, "Federal Racial Discipline Quotas Create
     Chaos in St. Paul Schools," *The Federalist*, July 29, 2016, http://
     thefederalist.com/2016/07/29/federal-racial-discipline-quotas-
     create-chaos-in-st-paul-schools/.

4   "The Diversity Delusion (Heather Mac Donald Interview)," *The
     Rubin Report*, January 23, 2019, https://omny.fm/shows/the-rubin-
     report/the-diversity-delusion-heather-mac-donald-intervie.

5   "The Diversity Delusion."

6   John Stonestreet, "Good Families Are Unfair?" *BreakPoint*, The
     Colson Center for Christian Worldview, May 20, 2015, https://
     www.christianheadlines.com/columnists/breakpoint/good-
     families-are-unfair.html.

7   Stonestreet, "Good Families Are Unfair?"

8   Rebecca Klar, "Pressley: Democrats Don't Need 'Any More Black
     Faces That Don't Want to Be a Black Voice," *The Hill*, July 14, 2019,
     https://thehill.com/homenews/house/453007-pressley-democrats-
     need-any-more-black-voices-that-dont-want-to-be-a-black.

9   Philip Carl Salzman, "How 'Social Justice' Undermines True
     Diversity," Minding the Campus, March 25, 2019, https://
     www.mindingthecampus.org/2019/03/25/howsocial-justice-
     undermines-true-diversity/.

10   Rod Dreher, "No Traditional Christian Doctors Need Apply,"
     The American Conservative, July 23, 2019, https://www.
     theamericanconservative.com/dreher/no-traditional-christian-
     doctors-need-apply/.

11   See Scott D. Allen and Darrow L. Miller, *The Forest in the Seed: A Biblical Perspective on Resources and Development* (Phoenix, AZ: Disciple Nations Alliance, 2006).

12   See Genesis 1:28.

13   For more on these biblical truths that should shape our approach to fighting poverty, see Darrow Miller's book *Discipling Nations: The Power of Truth to Transform Cultures*, 3rd ed. (Seattle, WA: YWAM, 2018).

14   Burgess Owens, "I Didn't Earn Slavery Reparations, and I Don't Want Them," *The Wall Street Journal*, May 24, 2019, https://www.wsj.com/articles/i-didnt-earn-slavery-reparations-and-i-dont-want-them-11558732429.

15   Romans 13:1–7.

16   Exodus 20:1–17.

17   Kaufmann Kohler and William Rosenau, "Covetousness," *Jewish Encyclopedia*, 1906, http://www.jewishencyclopedia.com/articles/4715-covetousness.

18   For more on this topic, I recommend a previous book I wrote with my colleagues Darrow Miller and Gary Brumbelow: *Rethinking Social Justice, Restoring Biblical Compassion* (Seattle, WA: YWAM, 2015).

19   Ben Shapiro, "How the West Changed the World for the Better," *National Review*, March 19, 2019, https://www.nationalreview.com/2019/03/western-civilization-revelation-reason-worth-defending/.

20   Christina Hoff Sommers, "The Threat to Free Speech," American Enterprise Institute, January 22, 2017, https://www.aei.org/articles/christina-hoff-sommers-the-threat-to-free-speech.

21   Howard Zinn, *A People's History of the United States*, quoted in History Is a Weapon, https://www.historyisaweapon.com/defcon1/zinnkin5.html.

22   Ta-Nehisi Coates, "The Case for Reparations," *The Atlantic*, June 2014, https://www.theatlantic.com/magazine/archive/2014/06/the-case-for-reparations/361631/.

23   "John Winthrop's City upon a Hill, 1630," Mount Holyoke, https://www.mtholyoke.edu/acad/intrel/winthrop.htm.

24   Bo Winegard, "Progressivism and the West," *Quillette*, March 9, 2019, https://quillette.com/2019/03/09/progressivism-and-the-west/?utm_source=Intercollegiate+Studies+Institute+Subscribers&utm_campaign=c8042586e9-Intercollegiate+Review+March+21+2019&utm_medium=email&utm_term=0_3ab42370fb-c8042586e9-93107593&goal=0_3ab42370fb-c8042586e9-93107593&mc_cid=c8042586e9&mc_eid=addf900d03.

25   See, for example, Brian Fikkert, *Becoming Whole: Why the Opposite of Poverty Isn't the American Dream* (Chicago: Moody Publishers, 2019).

26   See, for example, Patrick Deneen, *Why Liberalism Failed* (New Haven, CT: Yale University Press, 2018).

27   Walter Olson, "Yale and the Puritanism of 'Social Justice,'" *The Wall Street Journal*, March 6, 2018, https://www.wsj.com/articles/yale-and-the-puritanism-of-social-justice-1520381642.

28   "Murder of Laquan McDonald," *Wikipedia*, https://en.wikipedia.org/wiki/Murder_of_Laquan_McDonald.

29   "Homicides in Chicago: A List of Every Victim," *Chicago Sun-Times*, https://graphics.suntimes.com/homicides/.

30   See Darrow Miller with Stan Guthrie, *Nurturing the Nations: Reclaiming the Dignity of Women in Building Healthy Cultures* (Downers Grove, IL: IVP Books, 2008).

31   Tracey Wilkinson, "Why My Patients Will Suffer under Trump's New Birth Control Rule," *Vox*, October 12, 2017, https://www.vox.com/first-person/2017/10/12/16464204/patients-suffer-trump-new-birth-control-rule.

32   Frederica Mathewes-Green, "When Abortion Suddenly Stopped Making Sense," *National Review*, January 22, 2016, https://www.nationalreview.com/2016/01/abortion-roe-v-wade-unborn-children-women-feminism-march-life/?fbclid=IwAR0Pn9FMG8NQBOt9-ZRsKQITf0GxZqWKf3T0c6nv4vP3XysmN0YjzYI3VW4.

33   Andy Stanley, "Why Do Christians Want to Post the 10 Commandments and Not the Sermon on the Mount?" *Relevant*, January 7, 2019, https://relevantmagazine.com/god/why-do-christians-want-to-post-the-10-commandments-and-not-the-sermon-on-the-mount/.

34   Fr. Mark Hodges, "U.S. Episcopal Diocese Votes to Stop Using Masculine Pronouns for God," *LifeSite News*, February 1, 2018, https://www.lifesitenews.com/news/u.s.-episcopal-diocese-votes-to-stop-using-masculine-pronouns-for-god1.

35   Trent Horn, "'God Made Me Gay,'" *Catholic Answers*, April 11, 2019, https://www.catholic.com/magazine/online-edition/god-made-me-gay.

36   David Gibson, "Oberlin bakery owner: Gibson's Bakery paid a high cost for an unfairly damaged reputation," *USA Today*, June 21, 2019, https://www.usatoday.com/story/opinion/voices/2019/06/21/oberlin-college-gibson-bakery-lawsuit-column/1523525001/.

37   Joe Carter, "The FAQs: What Christians Should Know about Social Justice," The Gospel Coalition, August 17, 2018, https://www.thegospelcoalition.org/article/faqs-christians-know-social-justice/.

Chapter 7

1   As quoted in Scott Allen, "History Repeats Itself," *WORLD*, January 12, 2019, https://world.wng.org/content/history_repeats_itself.

2   William McLoughlin, *Modern Revivalism: From Charles Grandison Finney to Billy Graham* (Eugene, OR: Wipf and Stock, 2005).

3   As quoted in Allen, "History Repeats Itself."

4   Jorey Micah, "The Rise of Evangelical Feminism," *Relevant*, March 29, 2016, https://relevantmagazine.com/god/rise-evangelical-feminism/.

5   As quoted in "Black Feminism, the Black Conscious Community and the Black Church by Demetrius Dillard," *Northend Agent's*, March 21, 2017, http://www.northendagents.com/black-feminism-black-conscious-community-black-church-demetrius-dillard/.

6   As quoted in Jorey Micah, "The Rise of Evangelical Feminism."

7   Marshall Kirk and Hunter Madsen, *After the Ball: How America Will Conquer Its Fear and Hatred of Gays in the 90s* (New York: Plume, 1990).

8   David P. Gushee, "On LGBTQ Equality, Middle Ground is Disappearing," *Religion News Service*, August 22, 2016, https://religionnews.com/2016/08/22/on-lgbt-equality-middle-ground-is-disappearing/.

9   Rod Dreher, "We Have Been Warned," *The American Conservative*, August 23, 2016, https://www.theamericanconservative.com/dreher/we-have-been-warned/.

10 Rachel Held Evans, *Searching for Sunday: Loving, Leaving, and Finding the Church* (Nashville: Thomas Nelson, 2015).

11 "racism." Merriam-Webster.com. 2020. https://www.merriam-webster.com (June 3, 2020).

12 Douglas Murray, *The Madness of Crowds: Gender Race and Identity* (London: Bloomsbury Continuum, 2019), 127.

13 Andrew Sullivan, "Is There Still Room for Debate?" *New York Intelligencer*, June 12, 2020, https://nymag.com/intelligencer/2020/06/andrew-sullivan-is-there-still-room-for-debate.html.

14   "Civil Rights," *Democrats.org*, July 2, 2020, https://democrats. org/where-we-stand/the-issues/civil-rights/.

15   Robert VerBruggen, "Trends in Unmarried Childbearing Point to a Coming Apart," *Institute for Family Studies*, February 20, 2018, https://ifstudies.org/blog/trends-in-unmarried-childbearing-point-to-a-coming-apart.

16   Walt Blackman, "Abortion: The Overlooked Tragedy for Black Americans," *Arizona Capitol Times*, February 25, 2020, https:// azcapitoltimes.com/news/2020/02/25/abortion-the-overlooked-tragedy-for-black-americans/.

17   African-American Family Structure (July 2, 2020). In Wikipedia. https://en.wikipedia.org/wiki/African-American_family_ structure.

18   Andrew Sullivan, "Is There Still Room for Debate?" *New York Intelligencer*, June 12, 2020, https://nymag.com/intelligencer/ 2020/06/andrew-sullivan-is-there-still-room-for-debate.html.

19   Dakota Smith and David Zahniser, "LA police union, angry over Garcetti's 'killers' comment, calls mayor 'unstable,'" *Los Angeles Times*, June 5, 2020, https://www.heraldmailmedia.com/news/ nation/la-police-union-angry-over-garcetti-s-killers-comment-calls-mayor-unstable/article_27c3b685-35ac-58d2-8c10-f68fcc0b99a3.html.

20   Steven W. Thrasher, "Police Hunt and Kill Black People Like Philando Castile. There's No Justice," *The Guardian, US Edition*, June 19, 2017, https://www.theguardian.com/commentisfree/ 2017/jun/19/philando-castille-police-violence-black-americans.

21   Ben Crump, "I Believe Black Americans Face a Genocide. Here's Why I Choose That Word," *The Guardian, US Edition*, November 15, 2019, https://www.theguardian.com/commentisfree/2019/ nov/15/black-americans-genocide-open-season.

22   This was the number listed on May 1, 2020. https://www.washington post.com/graphics/2019/national/police-shootings-2019/.

23　Peter Kirsanow, "Flames from False Narratives," *National Review*, June 4, 2020, https://www.nationalreview.com/corner/flames-from-false-narratives/.

24　Jan Jekielek, "How The Tragic Killing of George Floyd Has Been Exploited," *The Epoch Times*, June 6, 2020, https://www.theepochtimes.com/how-the-tragic-killing-of-george-floyd-has-been-exploited-bob-woodson_3379519.html.

25　Andrew Sullivan, "Is There Still Room for Debate?" *New York Intelligencer*, June 12, 2020, https://nymag.com/intelligencer/2020/06/andrew-sullivan-is-there-still-room-for-debate.html.

26　Eric Mason, *Woke Church: An Urgent Call for Christians in America to Confront Racism and Injustice*, (Chicago: Moody, 2018), 66.

27　Ibid.

28　Ibid.

29　Ibid.

30　Ibid.

31　Ibid.

32　Ibid.

33　Ibid.

34　Ibid.

35　Ibid.

36　Ibid.

37　Ibid.

38　Ibid.

39　Ibid.

40　Ibid.

41　Ibid.

42　Other evangelical supporters of ideological social justice include Ken Wytsma, lead pastor at Village Church in Beaverton, Oregon, founder of the influential Justice Conference, and author of the 2017 book *The Myth of Equality: Uncovering the Roots of Justice and Privilege.* In this book, Wytsma affirmed the concepts of unconscious racism, white privilege, and black liberation theology. His repackaging of social justice ideology for an evangelical audience was commissioned by InterVarsity Press. A glowing review of the book was published by The Gospel Coalition's Jessica Hong and Chris McNerney. They called the book "essential reading for every American evangelical Christian."

Another evangelical advocate of critical race theory is Dr. Christena Cleveland, director of The Center for Justice and Renewal, formerly a professor at Duke University Divinity School. Cleveland is a prolific writer and speaker. One of her articles is titled "Why Jesus' Skin Color Matters." Elsewhere Cleveland has written, "I've been wanting to dive deeper into an intersectional exploration that examines both God's blackness and femaleness on the cross." *Christianity Today,* for decades the flagship magazine of the evangelical movement, regularly publishes articles by Dr. Cleveland.

Thabiti Anyabwile, pastor of Anacostia River Church in Washington, DC, and regular contributor to The Gospel Coalition website, is yet another evangelical proponent of the Revolutionary Race Narrative. Speaking of the assassination of Martin Luther King Jr., Anyabwile stated, "My white neighbors and Christian brethren can start by at least saying their parents and grandparents and this country are complicit in murdering a man who only preached love and justice." How were they complicit in the murder of a person most of them had never even met? Because they were white. Collective guilt based on skin color isn't biblical justice, but ideological social justice.

Yet another prominent evangelical voice supporting critical race theory is Latasha Morrison, author of *Be the Bridge: Pursuing God's Heart for Racial Reconciliation.* Her course "Whiteness 101" teaches white evangelicals to "(1) develop their white identity,

(2) acknowledge their white privilege, (3) overcome their white fragility, and (4) recognize white supremacy." None of this comes from the Bible. All of it is sourced in academic critical race theory and whiteness studies. And yet, it is being promoted by mainstream evangelical gatekeepers such as *Christianity Today*.

43   Mason, 116.

44   "Shock Report: 46% of Young Americans Believe U.S. is More 'Racist' Than Other Nations," *Flag USA*, November 1, 2018, https://www.flagusa.org/s/FLAG-Patriotism-Report-11132018.pdf.

45   Sam Hailes, "Deconstructing Faith: Meet The Evangelicals Who Are Questioning Everything," *Premier Christianity*, April 2019,   https://www.premierchristianity.com/Past-Issues/2019/April-2019/Deconstructing-faith-Meet-the-evangelicals-who-are-questioning-everything.

46   Owen Strachan, *The City of God Podcast*, https://toppodcast.com/podcast_feeds/the-city-of-god-podcast/.

47   Statement on Social Justice and the Gospel, https://statementonsocialjustice.com/.

48   John MacArthur, "The Injustice of Social Justice," *Grace to You*, September 7, 2018, https://www.gty.org/library/blog/B180907/the-injustice-of-social-justice.

49   Statement on Social Justice and the Gospel, https://statementonsocialjustice.com/.

50   Phil Johnson, "Against Mission Drift," PyroManiacs, February 11, 2016,   http://teampyro.blogspot.com/2016/02/against-mission-drift.html.

Chapter 8

1   Barrett Wilson, "I Was the Mob Until the Mob Came for Me," *Quillette*, July 14, 2018, https://quillette.com/2018/07/14/i-was-the-mob-until-the-mob-came-for-me/.

2   Karlyn Borysenko, "After Attending a Trump Rally, I Realized Democrats Are Not Ready For 2020," *Medium*, February 11, 2020, https://gen.medium.com/ive-been-a-democrat-for-20-years-here-s-what-i-experienced-at-trump-s-rally-in-new-hampshire-c69ddaaf6d07.

3   Nathanael Blake, "I Didn't Vote For Trump in 2016; Here's Why I Hope He Gets Four More Years," *The Federalist*, February 18, 2020, https://thefederalist.com/2020/02/18/i-didnt-vote-for-trump-in-2016-heres-why-i-hope-he-gets-four-more-years/.

4   Wilson, "I Was the Mob Until the Mob Came for Me."

5   Scott Aniol, "What's Wrong with the Recent Evangelical 'Social Justice' Movements?" *Christian Post*, September 3, 2018, https://www.christianpost.com/voice/whats-wrong-with-the-recent-evangelical-social-justice-movements.html.

6   As quoted in Darrow L. Miller, Bob Moffitt, and Scott Allen, *God's Unshakable Kingdom* (Seattle, WA: YWAM, 2005), 32.

7   As quoted in an interview by Tim Stafford in "Mere Mission," *Christianity Today*, January 5, 2007, https://www.christianitytoday.com/ct/2007/january/22.38.html.

8   Stott, *Issues Facing Christians Today*.

9   Gunn, "Making Waves," 13.

10 John Stonestreet and David Carlson, "'Emanuel': The Untold Story of the Charleston Shooting," *BreakPoint*, June 12, 2019, http://www.breakpoint.org/breakpoint-emanuel/.

11 "Guideposts Classics: Corrie ten Boom on Forgiveness," *Guideposts*, November 1972, https://www.guideposts.org/better-living/positive-living/guideposts-classics-corrie-ten-boom-on-forgiveness.

12 Nancy Pearcey, *Total Truth: Liberating Christianity from Its Cultural Captivity* (Wheaton, Crossway, 2008), 58.

13 Koukl, 155.

INDEX

ABOUT THE AUTHOR

Scott has spent his entire career in the area of Christian community development, poverty alleviation, and justice ministry. His passion is to help Christians understand the biblical worldview as the only sure foundation for healthy, flourishing lives, communities, and cultures.

He is cofounder and president of the Disciple Nations Alliance, an international discipleship ministry that exists "to equip the Church to rise to her full potential as God's principal agent in restoring, healing, and blessing broken nations." The DNA is active in more than 100 countries worldwide.

After serving with the international development organization Food for the Hungry International for 19 years in both the United States and Japan, Scott teamed up with his friends and mentors, Darrow Miller and Bob Moffitt, to launch the Disciple Nations Alliance in 2008.

Scott is married to Kimberly and is a proud homeschool father to his five beloved children. He currently lives in Phoenix, Arizona.